Walking Naked
Survival of a Shattered Soul

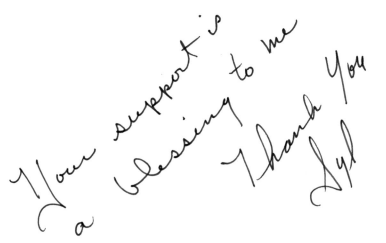

Your support is a blessing to me Thank You
Syl

Sylvia Hess

Walking Naked

ISBN: 0-9656867-0-1
Library of Congress Cataloging-in-Publication Data available

Printed by
Gilliland Printing
215 N. Summit
Arkansas City, Kansas

Walking Naked

.

Dedication

I dedicate this book to Dalton, the newest member of our family. (I've called him "Dalton Do" since he was born.) He was born August 18, 1994, to our youngest daughter and her husband. When he came to us, he made my heart care again.

This may seem strange to some and foolishly grandmotherly to others, but he represents to me an unstained hope. The rest of us in this family have been scarred for life by the hardships of the past few years. But he, for the time, is our unsullied little star. He will come to know pain at some point in his life but for now he is our bright new penny. His loyalty hasn't been tried, his heart hasn't been broken, his trust is at the highest level. His capacity for love is endless, the generous smiles he graciously showers on us are without blemish, and with all of these attributes he gives us an example to follow.

We can take our cue from him and strive to show loyalty, give with a generous heart and trust without question. Let our love be as innocent as his and may our smiles be gifts to one another.

I also want to dedicate this book to our dear son Keith, our son-in-law Wayne, and friends Brian and Katie.

Preface

As this piece of writing began to emerge as a book, I knew instantly that the title was to be "Walking Naked." If the words were to be read by many, I would be exposed to judgment by some. My mind, heart and my very soul would be on display.

When I thought about the possibility of being read by friends and family I had moments of fear and panic. I wanted to pull what I had written back to the safe anonymity of the time when only I knew its content.

My heart says, if the writing will be of aid to someone who is where I've been, I'll take the risk and let the opinions fall where they may.

So, I've come to terms within myself that I am "walking naked" before you in this book.

Walking Naked

Prologue

April 19, 1995

Holy Spirit, guide my words:

Last evening I went with friends to Wichita to a support group called "Survivors of Suicide." It was a profound experience for me. Being in a group of about twelve people who were all in the early stages of mourning someone who committed suicide was an extreme trial for me. I realized how far I've come, but more than that, I felt their pain as though it were my own.

I've gone through life very blessed. I have not been touched often by another's pain and even though I may have been extremely sorry for someone's trouble, I was still removed. Not so with these people. I know right where they are, standing alone, and their brokenness is mine. As the kids say, "I own it."

I wanted to gather up each of their sorrows into the car and take their wounded souls home to care for until they were well again. I know each of them must walk this devastating road alone but I yearn to hold their hands along the way. They are each one precious in my heart and that God has given me this, another gift, I am grateful. He has led me again to where He wants me to be.

This morning I am compelled to take up this "healer" that He has given me, my pen and paper. When my son died I was given this gift of needing to write. I live in a remote area and had no friends here. I was desolate and had nowhere to lay my pain. Through pen and paper, Christ allowed me to lay my broken soul at His feet. So now I want to come to you with what I pray will be a healing experience. Healing doesn't come in a day or in a year or in any "time frame." We don't know the hour or day when we will realize we have healed.

Last night I wanted to tell each of these people that, only a week ago, I first heard the birds again sing in the morning. That now I can be around "normal" people and even enjoy them. I am convinced that in this lifetime a remnant of this pain will always remain. At the same time, I also know I want to never forget it. It has cleansed me of false beliefs and standards.

Just as I learned something in each day behind me, I pray that each day to come will bring more light to my knowledge. Where I am today I will not be tomorrow, but I have passed many barriers and want to tell you about them.

Almost from day one I began to write. This morning I got out writing from the early days and read through it. Even then, I think, I knew I was writing to you.

A lot of it makes no sense and is the writing of someone who was insane. The experts say, "You will THINK you are going insane." Back up friend, I was insane. I knew it even then.

My gift to you is that I am living and am happy again and want you to know this. Now I am going to give you my first (I think, about) three months.

It's everything you are feeling now. I would like for you to know I survived, and how.

Walking Naked

I

In an instant, there was a cavern
where once had been a life

This Page Has To Be Written

Mrs. White (my sixth grade teacher) would not at all approve of the title of this page, but then she also thought we all ought to walk on the balls of our feet. As ludicrous as that teaching was, I had been taught to accept what my teachers said as being the gospel truth. I tried it, it didn't work.

This too, is beyond my conception. *My child can't be dead.*

My dear and precious son, Keith Leroy Hess, is dead.

He hanged himself in jail.

This is now written on my life.

Lord, please hide this page from me.

This is Day 8 since Keith died and we are still alive.

The fear is still alive and well. *"Blessed are they that mourn, for they will be comforted."* The truth of this has been proven. Shock should be able to be canned. Its numbing effect is a miraculous commodity.

This journal, if it continues, will be intended to keep my sanity, to maybe someday show my future family that we were real people, to say to others that survival is possible. I hope I will be able to say what is true and maybe even show the good side of life.

I think today is Tuesday, August 3, 1993. It may be another date, but accuracy is not a priority now. Geraldo is exposing someone else on the TV. Bill's gone to work, the geese are in the garden cleaning up the mess. You know how messy a vegetable garden gets in August. Ginger Dog just wants my attention and my world is void of humans. Maybe I will heal.

My goals are to each day make the bed, do the dishes and laundry, take a bath and, most of all, not let this pain harm others. The reality that I will not see Keith again in this life struggles with the reality that I will not have to fear and worry about what he will do next.

9:50 Went out and got the geese into the garden. Two followed me in and one stayed out. Bill put their water tank (a cement trough) in the garden this morning, so they were thirsty. Even with the gate open, all the geese would not go in. I practically had to crawl into the tank with them to get them to drink. They seemed to prefer the seed off of the grass to eating what's left in the garden.

Got what I'm sure will be the last of the corn. Bill's garden is usually so good, but it's just too much work for him this year. Back to the one independent goose. The others wouldn't settle down without her. I got a pail of water (I knew it hadn't drunk yet), and enticed it into the garden. So they are content for now.

Connie called.

Future reminders to myself, when someone else has a death in the family:

Rule 1 I will always put my return address on any communication. Often there was something in another's words that touched my heart and I wanted to respond. But looking back through the cards for a certain address was a great task (for me, at the time) and often very frustrating.

Rule 2 I will not send flowers unless I absolutely cannot think of anything else to do. Cut flowers that can easily be disposed of would be nice, and I will deliver them myself.

I've given away all that anyone would take and there are still three plants that need to go into the flower bed. I don't know if I will be able to get them there.

Rule 3 I can send a favorite or comforting Scripture along with a card. Deuteronomy 33:27 and Psalm 91 came from friends and they helped.

Rule 4 It is important to go to the funeral if possible. It means more than we can realize at the time.

Rule 5 If possible, take any of the following to the grieving family:
- Plain, small stationery for thank you notes
- Paper plates, cups, napkins, plastic forks
- A cooler of ice
- Disposable food containers
- Stamps

10:00 Grief without faith must be hell.

11:50 Bed is made, dishes are done. We've got a victory.

12:19 A few weeks ago I let go of my yearning for Keith to get well. I realized that there was no ability in him to know the difference between right and wrong. He was obsessed with a drive to self-destruct. There was a battle between his mind and heart. He was driven to possessive behavior toward his wife and children, by a heart that was so broken and scattered there was no hope of it mending, and his mind could not out-run the tortured heart.

The point is that God did what he promised. I had prayed for Keith's safety for a long time and had known that I was being answered. The night he died I knew that God had decided that the answer to those prayers was that Keith's only path to safety was to place him with Him. This is acceptable to me. I shake as I say this and my mind bleeds, but it is true.

Bill, I think it's called depression. I know it's called depression. When I'm there, please come sit quietly with me for awhile, but don't let me stay. It is a way to escape the pain and is very effective. It's a place to go that doesn't let anything touch you. That's good and sensible for awhile, but no joy gets past either. I apologize for going and plead with you to come get me.

12:48 Guilt is self-pity.

I vacuumed the sewing and utility rooms.

12:49 Adam + Eve = Mankind. After the fall, God left two (supposed) punishments: 1. Death 2. Work

My knowledge is just a speck of dirt on all the soil of this earth, but my soul knows that these are two of our most blessed treasures. We wonder and lament (gripe) about both. See how limited we are. We fail to see their value.

All that I've written is inside of me and I'm grateful to have somewhere to put it. This pen and paper are my best friends today. They "listen" with absolute, total and eager ears. We fell in love at first meeting this morning. I hope it is not just a "one-day stand" and they won't desert me tomorrow, but I have a feeling that this is where I'm supposed to be.

Bill, I finally found my broom! It was right where I parked it.

One half of kitchen vacuumed.

1:12 Ever since my friend Lois lost her son Brian, in an auto accident, I have known her pain. The night he died, my children (in their teens) came home at about 1:00 am or so and told me Brian was gone. I got up, dressed and went to their house. Lois was on the grass in the front yard, and I knelt down and said to her, "It will be OK." She looked up and said, "No, it will never be OK." I wanted to cut my tongue out and vanish. Then the pain came and it has remained with me ever since. I've not questioned it but wondered why I knew it.

God's gentle hand touched me eight years ago so I wouldn't be shocked so badly now. The pain I felt then wasn't there all of the time, but it was permanently marked on me. Another gift.

The rest of the kitchen swept, and three feet of living room.

1:32 Dear Lord, please let me not be defeated when Bill comes home. Also, thank you for teaching me long ago to accept what I cannot change. Amen.

When we receive these gifts of knowing do we bend to the floor to pick them up as though they were a precious pearl or do we pitch them in the trash like a piece of gravel tracked in by a visiting grandson?

1:43 Living room swept where furniture wasn't in my way. Bedroom, I don't care if it dies from dirt and falls through the floor.

1:50 A load of laundry started. I have to eat now, but it seems so unnecessary when I can still drink coffee and smoke. I wrote this lest you think I'm sane.

1:55 Ham and cheese sandwich.

Glenn, do not spend your time being angry for what Keith did. Spend your energy being thankful that you are sane. Along with anger usually comes an obligation of apology. Blaming what is impossible to blame on someone who can't receive or even conceive that they are wrong, is fruitless. Blame only belongs to someone who can own it. Keith could not. Anger only covers up your goodness and doesn't let it come out. You can't give to others when you are surrounded and smothered with anger. Let it pass away.

Insecticide on apples should be visible so you know when it's all washed off.

3:30 Took a bath

I started this day out with "Blessed are they that mourn." I've often wondered what that meant, not questioned, but just wondered. Now I think I know. He didn't just say that we would be comforted, but that we would be blessed. With that I go back to His sending a messenger angel to say to Mary that she would be *Blessed among women* and I take that to mean that she was #1, a 10, the best, the most wonderful of all. So my conclusion is that if we accept this word, "blessed" and look at its meaning, we have to acknowledge that this means we've been given something special. From this I also must conclude that along with this, my story, I must show Him some gratitude. And I think that gratitude should take the form of giving to others. A priest, confessor and friend once said "Never forget that each person you encounter is in some way having a hard time." That has been stuck in my mind. We all have little deaths and big deaths in our lives. Then sometimes we have the granddaddy of them all.

Our self-worth dies a "little death" after a snide remark or insinuation, even though we joke about it and try to laugh it off. "Medium deaths," we may share with a friend or just ponder, alone. "Big deaths," we are angered by, or hurt badly by, or learn from. Then some of us experience the death that humbles, crushes and debilitates. Only now can I accept and not blame. Only now can I appreciate and value the little, big and medium deaths.

Lord, protect me from the selfishness of my grief.

4:10 Clothes out of the dryer, bathroom mirror and shelves cleaned and deodorant applied. I think we're making progress here.

Keith's life was full of disappointments. Nothing was ever big enough to satisfy him. Nothing funny enough to feel the total joy of a big complete laugh. No love great enough to fulfill his craving to be loved. No gift expensive enough to be of value. No effort big enough to earn a grateful thank you from him. No food delicious enough to feel content with. No alcohol or drug strong enough to take away his pain. Knowing this as I do, I cannot wish him back to his joyless life. I am able to receive all these pleasures and cannot imagine life without them. Would I want him to die all over again?

4:35 I'm looking at the clock wondering when Bill will be home, and listening for his car.

Each step I put on the floor is in complete bewilderment.

Tomorrow maybe I can tell you about my other children. Maybe I can do my ironing. Maybe not.

Read Psalm 91 again.

4:44 Washed screen on little TV in kitchen, brought in rug.

4:45 A turtle is being harassed on the back step by the two kittens. Boy Cat has not been home for three days.

5:00 Let the geese out and they did their flying act for me. The black kitten, called Whitey, has become a predator. He is catching grasshoppers. Hurrah!

5:42 Called Virginia, worried that I haven't heard from her. Will the good death fairy please pick up the phone bill now. Matthew 25:1-13. How plain can it get?

8:50 Psalm 91:3-6. Bill got home around 6:00 and we talked. I fixed supper while Bill read what I had written today. As always he encouraged me. He said that what I wrote today made sense, so here I am again scribbling away.

Billy called.

During dinner Bill and I played our backgammon game and while I did the dishes, he did a little weed-eating. I went out to mess with the flowers a bit and, just as my heart was breaking again, he called to me to come look at the cows.

I took the geese to the creek for a minute and while there I wished for my son to have a clear creek to wade, a fishing hole that would give him a prize catch every time, a pond that would unfailingly produce bait for him and most of all someone to always be there to praise his catch. A dog to run with, and a friend to play with. Someone to brush his brow as he sleeps and someone to love him forever.

Today is about done and I can sleep to gain strength for tomorrow. On Day 1 I was afraid to go to sleep because I would have to wake up to the pain. Now sleep is a friend.

Good Night.

DAY 9

4:45 am   Coffee, toast and cigs.

5:00 am   With his permission, I will tell you Bill's horse story: Yesterday, when Bill left for work, he drove by the front pond and noticed our old horse was down. He stopped and yelled at her, hoping to rouse her. She did not respond to his call. Since he was late in leaving for Ark City, he just drove on.

During the day he often thought about her and the way she lay in the pasture. He assumed she was dead and had formed his plan for disposing of her body, getting the tractor, finding the chain, etc.

On his 35-mile drive home, he had decided to just look the other way when he passed her and ignore the whole situation. It was only his second day back to work. He had been one employee short (which makes a big difference in a four-man shop), so the work day had not been a good one. As he turned into the drive he couldn't help himself, and he turned to look her way. There she was, standing alive and well, grazing away.

The moral of this story: Even an old horse can make your day.

~ ~ ~

My day was made on Day 2.

That was the day I knew I would see my boy. My thoughts were scattered beyond belief. I was worried we would not get into town soon enough for me to see Keith and I was so frightened that he would be disfigured, that someone would say to me, "Maybe you shouldn't really look." I couldn't wait to get started. Somewhere, during the day, someone had called home to say he looked fine.

So that made me even more ready. By the time we got to town and I saw the mortuary, I was as excited as a child going to Disneyland. I couldn't wait to see him. We walked in and spoke briefly to Donna, the proprietor.

Where was he? Didn't they know how much I wanted to see him?

His dear face was so beautiful. Those tormented eyes were closed in perfect sleep. His face was clean and smooth without a smudge on him.

A little quirk of a smile on his lips that people have when they are content. This was the Keith I'd never known. This was the face I had always wanted to see. I couldn't help but to kiss, hug and run my hands over him. To tell him how proud I was of him, to say "I love you," to tell him everything was OK.

How could they tell me to leave when this was the Keith I had yearned and prayed for for so long? I wanted to bring this best of all Keith's home with me. Why would I need to leave?

Why do they want to put him in the ground? He is perfect and putting dirt on him will ruin how he looks. I can find somewhere to keep him. Please don't bury him.

Later that evening, the kids were all here at the house. There was a circle around me that separated me from the others. I fixed them drinks (which were needed), they called it "Mother's medicine." I could see the strain on their faces and wanted to take it away. If they had been young it would have been an early bedtime. Bill's hand was on my shoulder, even when he wasn't beside me.

Day 10

6:30 I got a broad, broad hint from Bill last night about the cookie jar that only had some store-bought cookies and a few old homemade left in it. So this day will soon begin to take its shape. I'll have to look back through the pages for my daily goals. Weren't they bed, dishes, bath and don't hurt any-one? This limbo I'm in is like a cocoon. Fuzzy, but the worries of yesterday have no bearing on today. I know I'm rambling, but this pad and pen have become that friend that you can rattle on with. I think I'll try to go back to sleep.

8:20 No sleep but went outside, cleared all the shoes away from the back step, emptied my wheelbarrow, watered and fed geese and chickens. The geese were a little wary of going back in the garden but that's where their water is, so they went. While I was outside they all stood on the garden step and discussed whether this was where they wanted to be.

Bill got up around 7:30. We *coffeed* a little while, then decided we would give ourselves a break and go to the dog races when we got the chickens cleaned. This being the first plan we've made, it felt pretty good.

It's difficult having to plan your day to balance your well-being. Before, days used to just happen. Now they need strategy and, hopefully, a plan that succeeds.

DAY 11

10:23 I've been planting the remaining plants. I divided the azalea into three plants and the big mum into five. So that is a good start on Keith's flower garden. I got some good dirt out of the big chicken house and hope that will help them. It is still only about 80° outside so I haven't shut off the attic fan yet, and closed up the house.

Well I might as well get down to it. I've been up quite awhile now and am still doing pretty well. I'm not an open bleeding wound yet, so that is a great improvement. Keith is riding on my mind like a red-winged blackbird on wheat. I've always wondered how they rode that easily on such a thin stalk. My mind is so fragile and yet he is still so easy on my mind.

Will I get angry? They (who?) say it's a stage we go through. Have all the mothers that have walked this path before me had to be angry with their dead sons? I hope not.

Glenn (son) and Duane (brother) called this morning. Glenn has shifted from angry to "*Why?*" We talked about the remodeling of their house for quite a while. He told me how much he has come to value family and how much he loves us all. What music to my ears! It doesn't get any better.

I suppose it's time to consider again those goals for today. My heart says, *Why bother?* My mind says, *You'd better bother.*

11:15 Cheese sandwich

I turned on the TV when I fixed my sandwich and it was sort of fuzzy again and I thought, *I'll have to ask Keith about it when I see him.* A jolt of electricity couldn't have shocked me more. I won't see him again, no no no.

11:25 I need to rest.

12:30 I'm going to bake some peanut butter cookies for Bill.

2:05 Cookies are done. I know it will get better. Lack of sleep really wears down the defenses. Being on guard all the time is sure the pits. As my grandson Terry sometimes says, "I don't think I'm having a good day."

I looked back to the goals. I did the dishes twice without making a grand announcement about it. Boy! Am I ticked off today.

The flowers look nice in the ground, it feels good with the windows open, I'm looking forward to Bill coming home, the cookies smell good and I'm grateful most of my work is done. I don't want to go to Wichita tomorrow. I want to look forward to something, something besides this craziness.

There is a soft breeze on my neck that ought to be given to someone else.

Fresh chenille off the clothes line, soft baby skin, warm sun in January, I hope he has it even better now.

Day 12

9:55 If I ever leave here again the first thing I'm going to do is buy a pen and pads of paper.

All of yesterday evening and this morning must have been assigned as "Guilt Day." We who have been given this position of grief should be furnished with a "Grief Calendar." Then when guilt jumps up at us from nowhere we could glance at the calendar and say "Oh, that's right, I'd forgotten this was a "Guilt Day!"

I could think of no time I'd ever done anything good or nice for Keith, only the harm. I still can't remember anything good, but the sense of harm is no longer as strong.

It's cool and raining which will be good for the flowers. The area I planted yesterday, from what I can see, looks good.

Last evening Brownie Goose attacked me. Then Mama Goose took him out, but good. He tried to make up with me all evening with little pecks and coos, but I really didn't care.

When someone dies of natural causes that is just what it says, natural. We expect old people's death and can even accept some young deaths - not many, but some. My greatest sorrow for Wayne, our son-in-law who died of brain cancer two years ago, was his not seeing his young son Loren grow up. Knowing he had seen the last Christmas with Loren that he would ever see just filled me with such sorrow.

~ ~ ~

Keith's death is threefold for me:
1. He is dead
2. He did it himself
3. In jail

No family with him as he died, no one to give him morphine for the pain, no one saying "We'll take care of your wife and children," no last hugs, no one to say, "It's OK."

No soft bed with one of those foam tuft mattresses, no soft lights, no cool washcloth.

My imagination says cold bars and rough rope. No house smells, only cold and dark.

No mother, no father, no wife, no children, no brothers and sisters. No last soft pats, just pain. Just someone who probably said, *Oh, shit.*
(No offense to the police officer who found him.)

I know God doesn't give us more than we can bear, but . . .

Through all our times of worry over the past two years, the local police were exceptionally good to all of us. They showed great patience and care toward Keith and often kept watch when we were unable to. I and my family are grateful for their diligence.

Today is a paper towel day. Tissues just can't handle the job, they are wimpy.

I want to talk about my other children, but they seem to be suspended somewhere. If I think about or talk about them, they might get hurt.

When reality is a nightmare, and I'm dead even when I'm awake, high noon is so crushing I don't know what to do or where to turn.

Back to the basics.

10:34 Going to make the bed.

10:55 Bed made and Glenn's sheets washing, upstairs picked up and closed up.

I don't quarrel with God's choosing to take Keith with him. I quarrel with my not doing my job well. I was given Keith to nurture and instruct, neither did I do well. Then my mind goes back to how different he was, so hard to handle. He communicated pretty well but there was always such sadness about him. Nothing was fair and everyone was always against him, he thought. I'm not trying to justify, just understand.

Is this a mystery? The church talks about mysteries a lot, maybe this is one. But God's business is His and He usually makes sense to me. This doesn't.

11:10 Jane called, electricity went off and it's still raining. Cats are on the porch, cozied up, and Ginger Dog will not even look at the door.

11:20 One shirt ironed.

This is like half a step into hell. Is there any escape or relief? So far I've stayed out of the pill bottle. There are Xanax left and I didn't take a sleeping pill last night and slept anyway.

I've read that pills are only a mask and you will have to suffer the pain sooner or later. Some of this pain may have to wait until later. The Xanax sure sounds like a good idea, whiskey sounds better. Thank God the peanut butter cookies don't look good.

11:40 Another shirt and pants ironed.

I'm afraid if I leave the house I'll never come back to the pain here. I always thought I was very efficient, get-the-job-done, no wimp about doing what needed to be done. This time I was frozen. Couldn't help with the funeral (except to say no preaching - be it priest or minister - and no canned music). I remembered his favorite color was blue, for his shirt. I did write the eulogy but otherwise (the hard parts) I couldn't do it. So much for being a "tough girl." The other children did it all.

Keith's eulogy was read by a friend. Here are parts of it:

Keith's illness was the kind that gives others symptoms also. When a brother's "broken soul" is the disease, we poor humans have no resistance against its malignancy. It spreads and feeds on our meager adequacies. We all fail to withstand it's weapons. Our hearts ache and our souls pray and our very selves are weakened. His sisters and brothers were always encouraged by any signs of renewed health and sorrowed by each new attack of this disease. There is a part in all of us that thanks God for allowing his pain to end. His torment has ended in the way God allowed, with mercy.

Please listen carefully and recall only the times you were given the grace to let love be the answer. Don't let your hearts remember the times we failed. The bad can be forgiven and forgotten but the good we must hang on to and cherish. God doesn't remember our sins so neither should we.

Listen now to God's prescription for life from 1 Corinthians 13:4-7:

Love is very patient and kind, never jealous or envious, never boastful or proud, never haughty or selfish or rude. Love does not demand it's own way. It is not irritable or touchy. It does not hold grudges and will hardly even notice when others do it wrong. It is never glad about injustice, but rejoices whenever truth wins out. If you love someone you will be loyal to him no matter what the cost. You will always believe in him, always expect the best of him, and always stand your ground in defending him.

From our friends we never heard a criticism of Keith; there was only sorrow and kindness in their eyes.

From his brothers and sisters, only honest pain that had love as its companion.

From his wife, an unwavering loyalty that went beyond any that we can imagine. Even after she had to part from him, her precious heart wanted only for him to find peace.

For his children there was true joy when Keith was able to join himself with them. Their tenderness and mercy were always unconditionally available to him.

From his father there was a yearning and a powerful desire to see Keith restored to what he knew Keith wanted to be. His willingness to help never, never ceased.

From his mother there was soft and ceaseless love that will continue through all of time and existence as we know it.

Our failures reach up to us at this time and pound on our hearts but, right after that, our love comes racing to chase away our pain.

God's mercy to Keith was a great sacrifice. For God to allow Keith to die in the way he did must have caused His heart to mourn. But in the end it was to let him come home to peace.

We should all hope and strive to let Keith go with a glad heart. Our guilt and pain are going to remain with us. But our plan is void in comparison with God's plan . . . so let's all allow God to have his way this time.

We will sorrow, we will anger, we will regret and we will question; that is our human frailty. But please, we ask that each of you who loves Keith so dearly, let joy, appreciation and pleasure cover over these painful ways - with giving ways. Bill and Sylvia along with all of you send Keith from here with joyful permission. As the Irish would say, "May the wind be at his back."

Please let Keith go with joy and ease. Let your hearts leave here with peace.

Two prayers, dear to the family, concluded the service, offering comfort and strength:

ANIMA CHRISTI

Soul of Christ, sanctify me; Body of Christ, save me; Blood of Christ, inebriate me; Water from the side of Christ, wash me; Passion of Christ, strengthen me; O good Jesus, hear me; Within your wounds hide me; Separated from you, let me never be; From the evil one protect me; At the hour of my death, call me; And close to you bid me; That with your saints, I may be, praising you forever and ever. Amen.

And to our Mother the Blessed Virgin Mary:

THE MEMORARE

Remember, O most gracious Virgin Mary, that never was it known that anyone who fled to your protection, implored your help, or sought your intercession, was left un-aided. Inspired by this confidence, I fly unto you, O virgin of virgins, my mother. To you I come; before you I stand sinful and sorrowful. O mother of the word incarnate! Despise not my petitions, but in your mercy hear and answer me. Amen.

Thursday, August 5, 1993

11:55 Another pair of pants ironed, no pills, no booze and all points south.

I always have joked about "gin in the afternoon." I've never done it. I wonder if Linda would like to go to a nice cool bar, where no one cares how ruthless a person can be on themselves. She would probably go into a dead faint at the suggestion.

Pen and paper are great, Tony-the-tiger "*Grr-r-r-reat!*" at conversation. No rejection of my thoughts or feelings. No denial, no correction. Total acceptance, its silence is truly golden.

from despair
he hung there

12:02 Another shirt ironed. Another battle done over life's wrinkles, dust, smudges, smears, stains, streaks. I can handle those. Where is the "Hints for Pain" section? Is there a society for crippled parents? I have many questions for them. Do I want to hear the answers . . .? No.

12:10 How do warmed over salmon patties sound?

I've looked out the window at his garden at least thirty times this morning. It's OK. There are three azaleas, five mums, a little ajuga and some sedum there so far. I want an ivy on the cellar wall and some flat rock from the creek to walk on to weed it, sort of an arched path. Again no argument from the pen and paper. I could tell them anything and they would accept it. "I went to the moon last week and shook hands with Father Time at the grocery store." This could be like playing house when

I was little. It's an escape. The pen and paper are great, but I think I'll keep on the up and up with them and not lie.

Sometimes each 10 minutes is an eternity and then three hours slip away. Working outside yesterday the time went fast, no outside work today; it's still raining.

12:50 One and a half lemons later, the salmon patties weren't that bad.

In my thoughts and perceptions of Keith, he is always a child. To me, he is a little boy, even at 36 years old. Would it be that way with the other four, or is it just because he never grew up?

Having electricity off doesn't affect the pen and paper.

I don't hear the geese chattering now, maybe they've gone to shelter somewhere. This silence is deadly.

1:10　Upstairs bed made.

2:30　Did he suffer?

I've always done my job. Can't remember hardly ever when I didn't do what I was supposed to do.

Bath.

3:15   Bath always helps soothe the heebie-jeebies.

5:35   Dinner. Got some onions out of the garden for hamburgers. Brownie Goose was very contrite and didn't try to eat me again.

A Gift For You, My Son

When we first began to run out of groceries, I realized that I could not stay in the cocoon of my home forever. I knew I had a decision to make. My impulse to hide said, Go to Bartlesville to shop, no one knows you there. The prying eyes and opinions will not be there, they are all in Arkansas City. We've had a business in "Ark City" for 25 years, which makes us visible. We raised five children here who were well known. We had no shrinking violets. Some excelled and then there was Keith.

I knew that running now to another town to shop would somehow degrade Keith and me, so I didn't. But I couldn't quite manage driving down the main street, so I took the adjacent one. My whole being was on fire with fear and determination.

I walked into the sandwich shop to meet my friends for lunch feeling like I was going to be eaten by the lions. In a way some of them did eat me with their stares and behind-their-hands talk, but some came to me to offer kindness. One woman came and said, "You look like you need a hug." How many times have we offered that hug, not knowing how valuable it might be.

This act was my badge of honor. Had I not done this I would have been turning my back on my son. Keith's importance would have been diminished and my shame would have been justified. My straight back and rigid composure said, *Keith was a valuable person and still is in my heart. It said, He was brave and a hero who harmed no one,* even though the blackness he endured wanted to hurt someone else for his pain. Maybe no one else heard what my demeanor was saying, but I did.

For me, the embarrassment was a false pride that had to be dealt with as "the enemy." I was not walking into that place to announce that my Keith had just graduated from Harvard, but to say that the lowest act of death did not erase his life to having no meaning. My grief is a tribute to his life.

August 6

8:20 I'm going to switch to accurate dates now because I can't continue to count each day as the number of days Keith's been dead.

Last night Bill came home talking up a storm. If you read what I wrote yesterday, you can hear everything he said. So we are running neck and neck. He can verbalize, I have to write it out.

I feel better about our daughter-in-law, Doris, and the kids. We talked last night and she is putting her house in order. Hurrah for her. I love her so much and my admiration for her is huge.

Right now I feel strong enough to go to the grocery store in Ark City but I think that could crumble easily. Yesterday I was consumed with grief, today I feel a little insulated against it. Bill and I agreed last night that we cannot go on as we are. We are helpless against this craziness but realize that to go on living we have to somehow figure out a way to get ourselves together. At least somewhat. We had a good evening and, again, I can't imagine going through this alone. Our need for each other is very intense.

8:40 Called Duane. He is going to find out how much a 4-wheeler will cost. I really appreciate having Duane for a brother. No questions, he just does it.

8:55 Geese are out, chickens are fed and it is a remarkable day. Laundry started and I'm drinking my second cup of coffee. I didn't have to force myself to do any of these things. We never appreciate just such a thing as being on automatic pilot. The list is endless of what we don't appreciate, God's mercy being at the top of the list. Last night I realized what a gift I've been given, in that I have no anger or resentment towards Keith. More than that, I know his mind and understand he was unable to live as the rest of us do. Seeing his illness as just that, an illness, truly allows me to let go of him. This is separate from the grief, but I do not have that burden of anger. God's mercy is there if we just look for it.

9:40 Just bought a 4-wheeler. How about that!

10:19 Maybe this will be a little bit of a diversion away from the hurt. I'll let you know later. No one can live in that total dark depression forever without losing their grasp on reality. We think we're so tough, when really we are so fragile. When you think of yourself as a mountain and are then forced to realize you are only a piece of dust to be blown about by the slightest breeze, it's not so much a shock as an enlightenment. Our "control" is nonexistent. It's a fairy tale we like to believe. My attitude toward life has always been, "Take the good and leave the bad," and I still think this is a good philosophy. Bill and I talked last night about having no control in this life, and the death of our son has made that truth more apparent than ever. It is very hard, now, not to be afraid of everything and everyone. There is such a fine line between total despair and the ability to see and love life as it really is.

Reality is the worst and the best. Only blind acceptance that God's plan is better than ours makes it bearable. Again the "mystery" of God.

11:15 Well, I've had my bath, dressed, eaten and done the dishes. I'm ready to go to town again. Not really ready, but I've never been too afraid of much and now I have to do this. My guardian angel had better call in some help.

Here we go!

7:54 When I got to town today without pen and paper, I felt like a one-year-old away from home without her "bankie" and pacifier. I had dreaded going to town like a trip to the dentist. Then I decided I don't need any more dreads in my life, so I went. All I met was love and kindness, and I remained OK through it all: Wal-Mart, Homeland, Graves Drug, Kim's and tea with Beth. I feel like a champion. But every trip seems like the first.

I needed to look at the calendar to remember the exact date of Keith's death, and then I folded. But, all in all, it was a good day. Acceptance is a true gift. It seems as though everyone I talk to has someone who is afflicted like Keith. I feel their pain so strongly. Your life is not your own with that fear of what such a person might do next. Often that uneasiness is there still, but I'm sure it will go away.

It's like putting your arm out in the car to protect the baby and the baby is 18 years old. We don't give up easily, do we?

I've quit seeing Keith's face so much and begun to feel more secure. Some of the raw wound is healing. Optimism is an option. We cannot linger too long in that consummate darkness and stay sane.

Lord, please keep safe your children of un-sane mind, here, or there with you. Amen.

August 7

9:30   Got up at 8:30, up a lot in the night, but went back to sleep; an improvement. Chores are becoming more automatic.

9:52   Bed made, dressed, laundry put away, house picked up. Unbelievable.

In my mind, at certain points, this journal has been directed toward someone who has also lost a child. I'm going to keep these writings for future members of our family. Therefore, I will start to explain people, happenings, and so forth.

Bill and I live alone, as the children have all established their own homes and families. Our children are: Glenn, Keith, Kimberly, Billy and Jane.

We live in southeast Kansas, throwing distance to the Oklahoma state line. We have 191 acres "more or less" (that is how the abstract reads).

Flower Story

11:30 The flower story is personal to me but needs some background.

Our daughter, Kim, son-in-law, Wayne, and their two children, Heather, 13, and Loren, 5, were living in Phoenix, Arizona. In early spring, 1991, Wayne was diagnosed with brain cancer and not expected to live longer than three to six months. At that time, we lived at the south edge of Arkansas City, Kansas, on an acreage. We had two houses on this property, about 40 feet apart. One we lived in, the other we used for a guest house, canning, sewing, etc. (I had wondered why in the world we had two houses. The older I get, the more I know that everything has its reason.)

It was apparent that Kim and her family needed to come home. Keith and Billy went out to Phoenix and brought the children to me, while Kim finished up their business and Wayne completed his radiation treatments. Then in about a month, one of Wayne's friends and his wife took our horse trailer to move them back to our guest house. In looking back, I see the next three months were suspended above the rest of the world as we knew it. I quit my activities, Kim didn't work and our world centered around Wayne and his illness. He was a lousy patient and caused Kim a weary road to travel. Yet he was lovable in his own way too. I feel very fortunate that he let me share in his last days and death.

The night he died all of our kids (except Glenn, who lives in California) were at Kim's house until about midnight. Jane stayed all night at Kim's. I think Wayne died about 2:00 am. Jane came into our room and said she thought Wayne had died. I went over and used the stethoscope, but found no sound. I waited quite a while before calling the mortuary because Wayne was to be cremated and I felt Kim should have some time with him. Dawn was just cracking when the hearse left with him.

When Bill's brother, Lawrence, died about a year before, friends had brought out a rose bush to plant in one of the flower gardens. Being Catholic, we said a Hail Mary and the Our Father when we planted it. (I hoped at the time that Lawrence's Lutheran soul wasn't offended.) The rosebush did not bloom.

About 6:00 the morning of Wayne's death, while everyone else was sleeping, I was in the garden between the houses, hosing off the walk. I was fussing somewhat at God about his needing Wayne or Wayne's need of him. Wayne was only 30 years old and left two children, and I was cranky in light of only about 2 hours sleep. Then I turned around, and there, jumping up at me were three perfect little roses on the bush. I knew that was my answer. I was being told in a soft, gentle way to mind my own business.

During the just-passed days of August 2, 3, 4 and 5, I've walked through what I can only describe as a living hell. The torment was only just bearable. Last evening, God gave me another beautiful sign. In these last dark days, I had scalped the flower bed along the north side of the house. I had cut the herbs back to the ground, pulled away the overgrowth of flowers and in general just played havoc with it. The wheelbarrow was full of this debris, sitting just outside the gate. Last night, as I walked outside to go feed the geese, in the barrow was a flower in bloom, one perfect pink flower. I thought, *Oh, no, God wouldn't do that again, would he?* I went on around back and closed up the geese and chickens. It was almost dark as I came back around the house to where I could see the wheelbarrow. There, shining for all it was worth, was the little flower. That plant had been totally eaten up by a swarm of grasshoppers. It was almost totally brown from lack of water and heat and the little blossom was at least five feet from the root!

I went to the flower, stroked it, dropped tears on it and looked at its perfection. I knew I couldn't separate it from its destiny just as I couldn't wish Keith back only to suffer death again. I couldn't preserve its beauty, only tuck it into my heart. God had given me a good day and a lifetime gift and memory. When I looked out the door for the flower this morning, Bill had emptied the barrow. The space where it had been was so empty. I know there will always be an empty spot now in my life. Though I do have a feeling God plans to help me fill it somewhat, in some way.

August 8

12:13 My friends, Virginia and Connie, will be here soon for a visit. I'm really anxious to see them.

6:00 Connie and Virginia just left. It was such a good afternoon for me. There is something so wonderful about being able to sit at the kitchen table with friends and share each other's lives. It is cleansing and gives new perspective to some issues, also confidence in places where it's needed. Bless you, Father, for friends.

Bill has been mowing all day but he'll be in soon. He came in for lunch with us and then went right back out. The time he's taken to mow today has probably been good for him. Not only has he had the grief, and worry about me, but also the cares of the shop. So a day in the sun, with all other cares put aside, has probably helped him.

Also, his tractor came today, old, but new to him. I was telling the girls today about how rejuvenating this place has been for Bill. While we were at the other house Bill had decided he was old and it was all over for him. He was even somewhat depressed. (He will deny that to his dying day, but he was.) This place has given him a new lease on life. He loves his cows, tractor, pasture, the whole shooting match. I am very happy for him and he's young again.

9:26 After Virginia and Connie left, Bill and I went for a ride. It was a pretty evening. We rode to Hewins and back.

It seems as though the pain and tears just wait until there is a lull to demand attention. We drove by Carmena's (her husband died the Thursday before Keith did), and I thought how fortunate in our grief Bill and I are. We have each other and her lifetime partner is gone. No one to share with, no one to tell you they love you and everything will be OK. No wonder that after a spouse dies, some people are receptive to dying themselves.

Another day survived, some of it good, some bad, but better than yesterday.

God ought to weary of us, but He doesn't. Ginger Dog wants in and I want my bed.

Monday, August 9

Yesterday got by me without my writing. I got up late, at 9:00 am. I'd been up during the night, having had a horrible nightmare, although it was true.

Doris and the kids came out. Bill killed three chickens (they're too big now to be fryers) and Doris and I fixed dinner. We made a chicken casserole and, about 4:00, Beth and Gene came out. We visited, ate dinner and played cards. It is so nice to have friends to talk to. I feel so compelled to talk about Keith, I hope I don't offend anyone.

Tonight I have to get the raccoon. He is eating all the dog and cat food and using my mums as after dinner mints. So about sundown the hunt will be on.

August 10

Progress is on-going, I'm cleaning out the fridge. It's not a pretty sight. Everyone is where they are supposed to be, Bill at work, geese in the garden and I'm shoveling out the house.

The pain just lies there like I ate a rock, a big rock. But around and beyond that is the same support I felt within minutes of knowing of Keith's death. God's arms are so strong. Especially when we know that even standing up without Him would be impossible. The tears are still plentiful. Coffee and cigs are still my morning answer to life. Don't confuse my knowing of God's support with any strength on my part. I know it so strongly because of my weakness. Up to this point, my faith has only been pragmatic. Common sense told me when I was five years old that God made the grass. I was so impressed with this knowledge that, from that point on, I've had total faith in His existence. Being a realist did not at all interfere with this conviction.

I do not hear voices, see visions or receive any physical contact from God. Sometimes though, since this has happened, I feel like a truth has been revealed to me, brought home as a fact. One thought that keeps running through my mind is that we do not have to reach a certain level in our spirituality for God to touch us with His mercy. Most of all we have to be open to receive it, available. No amount of time, study, learning, or striving to be good, permits God to enter truly into our personal lives. I think just believing is enough to save our souls. But only after our so-called control is taken away, and we realize how very helpless we really are, can we say yes to his perfect love. I've wondered in the past about the concept of dying, going to heaven, and praising God forever and forever. Having only dealt with humans so far, I've come to the conclusion that being around someone whom you have to praise constantly can be a pretty big trial - and boring to boot.

But when I felt - and feel - this constant uplifting, it is absolutely no problem to consider praising him forever. What we receive now and in heaven is enough. I had never directly felt God's personal love for me before.

I don't want anyone to misunderstand my motives in revealing this. This encounter with God has come at the worst time of my life. I have been given a gift of acceptance, I've seen His glory and am in total awe and more secure than I've ever been. Believe this as true. I can't tell you why it is OK that my son is dead, nor can I tell you why it is OK that he hanged himself in jail. I just know that it was, and is, God's way and it is sure and true.

My prayer life has not increased in the popular sense of taking time out to speak to God directly about a specific topic. As I work, play, think and ponder, it is almost a constant conversation. It's a more casual relationship than I've had with Him before. It's more like a new presence. Sort of like a new puppy in the house (no messes, though), a new friend, a new companion. My prayers are more like statements of realization than a pleading for something or someone, or a question of some sort. It is very comfortable and has no urgency to it.

My point in this writing is only to say that being receptive is important. You can't make God give you a gift or even force yourself to be accepting, but you can be receptive. Slow down, calm down the anxiety.

We do have a say in our lives: we can either accept life as it truly is or we can fight it with a vengeance. Believe me, that fight is without merit. Only when we die to self can we accept.

The moments, days, and years of this life are so fast, they are like watching a 50-yard dash. Preparation for this race is essential and paying attention to our goals takes constant awareness. But, in the end, it is over in a flash. Owning our own lives for what they really are is so tranquilizing. Knowing what I will be, accepting what I am, leaves me open to all the goodness of this earthly life. Not waiting until it somehow becomes perfect, perfects it. That was a gift Keith didn't possess. His ability to love was real. But his urgent, anxious and obsessive mind could not let life be for him as it really is. I've no doubt that he loved all of the people in this family and his friends, this is sure in me. But the fulfilling life was not here for him. I can only think of it as a gift that God's mercy accepted Keith as he was and not as we thought he should be. Only His perfect ways are enough.

I'm at a fork in the road and I have to make a decision. I can choose self-pity, questioning, hatred and despair, or I can accept His mercy, both for myself and for Keith. I can open my mind and heart and choose God's road, or I can go the other way. On the wrong road I will have to carry blame, anger and death, knowing these parcels will slow my step and eventually stop my walk and there will be a "Road Closed" sign in front of me. If I let my step go into that insanity where there is no light, only darkness, I will be robbed of all comfort and love.

Along either of these roads will be death or some sort of change - a child, a spouse, a sibling, a friend - but in taking God's road I will not end up alone. The other road offers no support, no give-and-take and certainly no mercy. Also that road has all that I fear: rejection, loneliness and eventual failure. I will be blind to the future on God's road, but have every hope of eternal joy at its end.

I've always had a fear of becoming a religious fanatic, one people talk about and criticize. This may happen, but it really doesn't matter to me anymore. I think I've let go of that vanity. To look upon these gifts of mercy and love and not accept them would be, for me, a serious sin. We accept material gifts and gifts of love from other humans with gratitude. No problem. But when it comes to accepting God's gift, I think the enemy tries to step in and say to us, *You are special enough that you don't need anything from anyone*. We look at God's charity as though we just went on welfare and don't want anyone to know about it. The enemy then wins and cuts us off from receiving what God wants to give us, freely (Mark 9:33-37). The enemy wants us to put up that false bravado that strips us of self-respect and makes us not love ourselves, God or others.

I have had the answer to that worst fear of all mothers: *What if I lost my child?* I now own that answer and am walking with it. At the same time, I can understand Christ saying on the cross, *"My God, my God, why have you deserted me?"*(Mark 15:34.) It was His final gift to us as human. It was not that He despaired of His Father; it was that He gave us a final acknowledgment that we will fail. In His very last words he gave hope to our despair. In our human fear that we will fail, we can look to those words. He knew there would be times when despair would be acted out in our lives. That God, on this day, has chosen to remove that despair from my soul is a perfect gift.

In Mark 14:36, The agony says that our human heart pleads to not be put through such pain, but that our will must be broken to say, "I want your will, not mine."

I can cry without despair, mourn without malice, wish that this would pass away without being unfaithful. But I cannot live without acceptance, hope and surrender. Those are the gifts God has given to me and they are the finest.

Even in those last hours and moments as a human, having taken on our humanity, He let us know that He had lived our pain and failures. He chose those last moments and words to be His last gift to us. To say, *I know, I have been you.* How can we say He doesn't understand, or blame Him for our pain?

Keith's taking of his own life proves to me the reality of his illness, and I know God accepted him with open arms. This may seem to be in direct conflict with what I have been saying up to now. You can say, "Keith took the wrong road and ended in black aloneness. He could not accept life's troubles. He gave suffering to many. He did not abide in God's ways." And I say "True. True. True. True." But saying "Why would God accept Keith?" is saying, "God judges us by my standards." But He has that unqualified love that Keith wanted so badly. We all, by our own standards, judged Keith to be wrong and at fault for not just straightening up his life. God's standard for judgment takes in all the pain in Keith's life, be it real or imagined. He takes all our afflictions and disappointments into mind, what is in our hearts. We must not limit Him to our small way of thinking. When we limit Him to our knowledge, we don't have to give up any of our power, worth, or thinking of ourselves as the beginning and the end. We are the limited ones, not God.

August 11

Sleeping pill last night.

The big goal today is to go to lunch. I'd rather wash all the windows in the house at this moment. I will enjoy it once I make myself do it. After dishes, bed and bath were accomplished I decided that burying myself here all week, going only to the grocery store, is self-defeating. So now I'm going to go to Tuesday lunch and club. It is good to have goals, as long as they are attainable. I'm going to try, for once in my life, to give myself some room. I tend to fill myself to the brim with things I have to do. I realize that all the "things" I do are a mislaid effort to be important to someone. I could only gain stature in my mother's sight by how much housework I did for her. I only then received praise, and often it was secondhand. Continuing this into adulthood was easy because I became a housewife. I've received a lot of pleasure from my homes but, at the same time, enough is enough. I don't say these things in an effort to say, "Poor me," but in an effort to put my priorities into their proper order. Staying home all the time is tipping the balance of the scales to one side too much. I enjoy my friends and rely on their support, so to deny myself is only a minus.

Giving myself permission to write is a biggie, too. I've always wanted to write but said to myself, *After my work is done I'll have a little time,* or *I'll write some this evening.* Those times never worked out. Either other things happened, work lasted longer than expected, or I was just too tired. Giving myself permission to write at any time is a great gift to myself. I enjoy writing, it spends my inward quarrels with myself, it is not difficult and, in many ways, it is a pleasure. I never lack for something to say to the pen and paper. It floods out of me at a rate that astounds me. My hope is that I can write something of value to someone else.

For a fleeting moment I decided that Keith wasn't dead, there was a mistake about who died and he was still alive. It took as long to realize that this wasn't true as it took me to write it. What a glorious few seconds! I saw him walking, and so alive and well. But my memory of who was in that coffin was too strong. My heart and resolve fell to earth. All of our false hopes do. These tears are coming from an overpowering sorrow that seems to just wait for its opportunity to grab me.

Sorrow is an entity unto itself, a power. Its life is separate from us, yet it controls.

It takes a great deal of concentration to leave the house.

7:34 Made it to Ark City for lunch with my friends. I enjoyed being with them but feel like a fish out of water. I suppose eventually I will feel at ease again out of my house, but I have a feeling it will be longer than I think.

As I came home, I ran into Jim, who was just beginning to cut Bill's hay. I came in and made meatballs and spaghetti sauce.

Billy and Randy (Billy's friend - and ours) have gone to Wichita to bring home the 4-wheeler. Bill has gone to the east hay barn to do a little cleaning, to be ready for the hay. So I've a little time before they are here to eat.

I've been shaky and down the last few hours. What a blessing our homes are, and I thank God mine is safe and without stress. I feel so insecure away from home. I know my attention span is much less now, and I really have to concentrate so I can get where I need to go. I feel sorry for Bill having to run the shop. I think his having to see so many people is more of a problem to him than the actual work.

How my mother-in-law, Della, must have suffered! Her daughter, Dorothy, was 23 years old. Just before Christmas, soon to be married, she was killed in a car wreck. We lost Della last October. She was such a nice person and now I understand even more why she would plead with Bill to be careful and take care of himself. When you lose someone you love, you become frightened for all the others. I will try to not do that. I used to always say to the kids when they left to go somewhere, "Have a good time." Now I want to scream and plead for them to be careful, but I'm going to try to still say, "Have a good time." I feel at times like I'm writing to great, great, great grandchildren and beyond. Although you are far removed in time, know that even now, I love you and am so proud of you. Please take care of yourselves and I pray for your safety. I can't imagine what your life-style will be, but know that already in 1993 someone loved you.

August 12

8:55 The boys brought the 4-wheeler last night. Bill left a little earlier this morning. I went out to do the chickens and geese, also to try to get the geese to follow me down to the creek on the 4-wheeler (me on the 4-wheeler, not the geese). They followed me about to the gate, then panicked and wouldn't go through the gate. I went through the gate and down the hill about 15 feet, then turned off the motor. I couldn't get it started, so I went back up the hill to call Billy.

9:55 I have to put it in neutral before turning off the motor. Lesson learned. I walked the geese down to the creek, came back up, did what Billy said and I was off again. Later, I rode down to the creek, visited the geese, then went up the hill and down to the dead end on the road to town. What a trip! I feel like I've crossed over a new land. Driving it was a little easier this time. Billy called back to check if I got it going. Dishes done, bed made, dog dipped and half of one of the cats. Not a bad start!

10:35 I went out and picked enough apples for a pie. We're not really sure they are ripe, so I'll make this pie to see. It just entered my mind that I ought to throw in some of my recipes; someone might use them. Most of my cooking is "kind of by a recipe" and that's as near as I can describe it. I'll try to give exact ingredients and go by the book, then tell you the next day if it was any good. I've put my ingredients for pie crust and all utensils I'll use in the fridge to chill. (Kim taught me that method. See, old dogs can learn new tricks.)

Pie Crust for two single-crust, or one double crust pie:
(This was my mother's recipe)

Mix with fork:
2 cups flour
1 teaspoon baking powder
dash of salt
Drop in globs on top of flour:
1 cup Crisco or lard

Chill in refrigerator at least two hours. (Kim leaves it overnight.) Take out of fridge, break up shortening into workable sizes. Use your hands to shred shortening into the flour. (This action is much like washing something out by hand, but work it only one way, not back and forth. Lift with fingers to shred against pads at base of thumbs.) Get it to about pea size on average; some will be larger, some smaller. Put back in fridge. Peel apples. Add about 1 1/2 cups sugar, about 3 tablespoons flour and 1 to 2 teaspoons cinnamon. Some apples need more sugar, some less. After you have sugar, flour and cinnamon on the apples and mixed, eat one. This taste will tell you if you need more sugar or cinnamon. It's a personal taste thing.

Take flour mixture from fridge. Stir four ice cubes into about 1 cup of water to chill it. Then start sprinkling about 2 tablespoons at a time onto the flour mixture, each time moving the mixture lightly with a fork to incorporate both. When this forms into a dough, pat it down with a fork to make it stick together. Divide into two parts and roll out half for the bottom crust. Put into pie pan and add apple mixture. Roll out second crust and place over the apples for top crust. Pinch edges together all around the sides to seal. Sprinkle with sugar and bake about 1 hour or so at 350° until crust is lightly browned.

I decide how many apples to peel by looking at them. Imagine your apples in the pie (I like to mound them high) and a look at unpeeled apples should tell you how many to use. Remember, they shrink.

I also made some baked beans to cook while the oven is hot with the pie. For a small amount, about three servings, I used (all measures approximate): 2 cups (1 can) pork and beans, 6 tablespoons ketchup, 1 teaspoon Worcestershire sauce, 1/4 of a medium onion, 1/4 cup loosely measured brown sugar, 2 dashes salt, and 2 spurts of Louisiana hot sauce. Start with this and add a little of anything you think it needs. Remember to taste, then add more of anything that is good to your taste and you can, of course, double or triple as needed for larger groups.

Then I made a marinade for 2 sirloin steaks.
1/4 cup olive oil
1/4 cup port wine with a little sherry
Fresh Herbs: basil, rosemary and tarragon.
Combine to make about half a fistful, lighter on rosemary and tarragon. Chop.
Put all together in sealable plastic bag with the steak and refrigerate. Turn often during day. Grill in the evening.

I have some fresh tomatoes to slice and maybe some potato patties. I will wait and see if Bill is starved or not, to decide about the potatoes. I have some onions and cucumbers in vinegar I will probably use too. I sound like I'm very busy but these things don't take long.

I find myself pushing the pain away when I think of Keith and going on to do something else. Maybe that's a little bit of the answer. Also throwing in a small prayer helps. By nightfall I get a lot weaker. I love to work but get into trouble if I stay at it too long. I have a minor muscle disease and it gets mad if I work too much. The weather is hot-hot, humid-humid, typical of August in Kansas. It's after 11:00 a.m. and the cutter hasn't come to start mowing hay. It's still too wet. The lawn by the house still has dew on top.

11:30 Love my 4-wheeler! Went down to the creek to check on the geese and noticed wood that Bill wanted burned. Came up to get papers to start it with and went right back to start a fire. One trip a day, on a "good legs" day, was all I could manage. Now two trips in five minutes! I think next trip down, I'll take a swim.

12:10 Cooked some starch and am going to go back to doing up Grandma Bradshaw's "linens." You future generations can blame your thick ankles on her, my grandmother on my father's side. When Phyllis and I drove to New York last fall to bring back her dishes and china cabinet, my cousin, Pat, gave me a box of Grandma's linens. I salvaged the best and, before Keith died, I was in the process of cleaning, starching and ironing them. So I'm back to the chore. I keep thinking that, every time I write that Keith is dead, either I will begin to believe it or some of the hurt will go away. So far, it's still the same each time I say it. So it's back to the linens. A lot of the crocheted ones were done by my mother and some by Grandma Bradshaw. I don't think that I have any of Grandma Holman's, mom's mother. Her household items were sold at auction. I could not bring myself to bid with strangers for my grandmother's things. We went out of town that weekend. When I die I want my children to take turns taking what they want. Kim bought me a book for listing which items go to each person and their history. I left it at her house but will pick it up later. That was a very thoughtful thing for her to do.

5:25 Pie and beans are in the oven. The mower must have broken down or Jim is through mowing. I haven't heard him for a while.

No mail today and no phone calls, a nice busy day. Tomorrow I will go to Ark City to buy groceries and go to Wal-Mart, and run errands in general. I think Bill is going to mow the inside yard tonight but with this heat he may be too tired.

I'm smelling pie.

Friday, August 13

Yesterday I was gone all day, so no writing.

First I went to the quilting group. They need help in getting the raffle quilt finished by November for the turkey dinner at church. I really enjoyed the quilting and hope I get to go again. Then I picked up my car (flat tire), went to Wichita and saw my brother, Duane, took some parts for Bill, called Jane and we went to look for wallpaper for her bathroom. Then she and I went to the grocery store. I appreciate her so much. On the way home I stopped and picked up cooking wines and bread at the bakery. I was so nervous and frightened coming home, but after I'd been here a while I was OK again.

The hay haulers just knocked to say they were leaving pretty soon. The cutter is still bailing. Bill is a nervous wreck about getting it into the barn. (I believe this is an ailment common to all ranch people.)

This morning I took Bill to work in Ark City so I got a little bit of a late start but still got a lot done. Did the laundry, made cookies and muffins, rested, and now I'm making potato salad. I think I'll have quite a bit of company this weekend. Janie, Billy, Ron and Doris are coming for sure, I think, and anyone else is welcome.

Yesterday and today have been sad and happy at the same time. The sadness underneath seems to be permanent. Bill and I wonder if the pain will ever lessen; maybe it won't.

I try to be positive but am haunted by how alone Keith was, how he died in such desperation. Why didn't I just stop by one day and tell him how much I love him? Then I think about how frightened we all were and search back for my feelings at that time. The circumstances were bad, but oh! how I wish I could tell him how much he means to me. I don't think I have any words to describe this constant pain. I wonder if I can endure this forever. I pray for relief. Some of the shock is wearing off, I think, but I'm not sure about anything.

Sunday, August 15

12:47 No time to write.

6:02 Existing in this vacuum, while behaving on the outside as though you were a real human being, is so oppressive. It's like having stale air surround you. You can still breathe, but with no fresh air. I still see beauty with no inspiration. I laugh with no real joy, it is muffled and far away from my heart. It's as if my smile is drawn onto my face, like a happy face. Oh, to really be able to smell fresh air, to feel water, to really feel a good laugh, to see and feel beauty in my soul. I am a puppet playing at being who I used to be when my world was safe. There is no safety net now. I'm on the edge and can't see the bottom. Who will God need next? Does He take from us till we can endure no more, till we lie down and die ourselves? Will I ever feel sunshine again? Will the fear build more walls around me; will I build the walls so thick and strong I can't be hurt anymore?

Does a soul get calluses? I've never known where my soul was; now I wish it had never been shown to me. I barely breathe for fear of what will come next. Yet it yearns to really feel life again. Maybe if I act normal on the outside long enough, it will penetrate to live inside me. Right now a stone is wrapped around my heart. Where there was light and appreciation, anger at times, a yearning to be more and do more, there is a closed door. It slammed shut at that midnight call. The light went out and I'm here in the darkness without the will to reach out and try to find a window to open. The fear is of more and more pain, but how could it be any worse? What's here now, I can't bear. I have no weapons to use against it. Books, TV, work, fun are like loose papers in the wind. I get hold of one and the wind comes and blows it away. As I reach toward another, it goes. There has to be some escape, somewhere. Sleep is not really a friend, more like a wave from someone you hardly know.

I've had my share of disappointments, sorrows, failures, and myriad other happenings in my life, but none ever killed my soul. There was always a will to go on, and there were still joys if I looked for them. Now I can look at what always meant joy for me and feel nothing. It's like light falling on a blind person's eyes.

I have no answers, I feel I've lost the battle. I've seen many people who thought they were defeated by some enemy in their life, yet recovered with amazing agility. Am I just weak or is some part of me smart enough to know it's over, and the enemy has won? Will the real me please stand up, and come claim this package. Give me just a sip of who I was.

These feelings are real and I put them on paper as fact. The only answer seems to be: Time. At least that is what I've been told. But I have recorded (in my mind) that those who told me that, haven't been here. Maybe someone who has been here told them. Hell has been described as a yearning to see God's face and knowing you never will. Maybe there is a correlation. To see Keith's face . . .

I have to walk away.

August 16

5:40   I have peeled apples all day! I picked all the apples I could reach on my ladder today and have peeled all that I picked. I just peeled, cored and sliced them into salt water, drained them and put them into plastic bags, sucked out the air and put them into the freezer. They will make good apple pie and cobblers this winter. I think I'll make applesauce next and freeze it too. Bill will have to pick the rest of them for me.

Today hasn't been so bad and I've pushed the demons in my mind away when they came near. I just can't handle all that pain every day. I know it's lying back there just waiting for me, but today I have kept it at bay.

Boy Cat came home yesterday after being gone for a very long time (I believe I mentioned somewhere back that he was gone). He has lost a foot and is bone thin. I've fed him about five times today and he cried for me to pet him each time I took apples out to the freezer. Maybe this will cure him of going off, but I doubt it.

The carpenters are back and putting a new roof on the back addition of the house. They are going to put windows and wallboard on the new porch and new ceilings in the dining room and pantry. Then I can go ahead and do those rooms. Both are going to be papered and that will make a great difference.

The weekend was full of people, the kids said 30 people came and went. I enjoy having people here. On weekdays there usually are no people around, so I really look forward to the weekends.

My hands sure ache from all those apples, but I enjoy seeing them go in the freezer.

For the next three days I have somewhere to go every day, so probably will not write much, but I'll try.

~ ~ ~

Tuesday, August 17

Having a tragedy in our lives makes us so sensitive to others and their pain. The father of pro basketball player Michael Jordan has been abducted and killed. Ordinarily I would just say, "how sad," and say a little prayer for them. Now I feel their agony.

Monday, August 23

2:25 I got up at 4:30 this morning and just now sat down to rest for the first time. I canned pizza sauce and apple butter and got the laundry done.

The carpenters are here filling in a doorway, pre-wiring and hanging wallboard. Over the weekend we went to Arkansas to see Phyllis and Jack. It was good to get away for a couple of days.

Yesterday on the way home I realized so strongly that I wasn't going to see Keith again. This sorrow seems to come at me like water rising on a drowning person, but only in amounts I can stand. I seem to have started building a wall against the grief. I cannot tolerate that much hurt all the time, so I've begun to push it away when it comes toward me. I don't know if this is a good or bad tactic, but I do know that I could sit down and cry for the rest of my life. I mean this literally. No amount of tears will ever ease this hurt. So maybe all mothers who lose a child begin to push back the hurt.

I saw Lois the other day and she assured me I'm not going nuts. Just being near her lets me know that we might survive this. This unexpected, gradual awareness of Keith's death almost annoys me. Just when I've hurt to the point of all I can bear, another thing comes screaming through my brain. If I'm going to be crushed, please do it all at once and get it over with.

That was a stupid statement. Not only would I be unable to handle it all at once, but I've begun to realize it will never be over with. I hope someday I can look at him with loving memory instead of looking at him as I do now. I keep seeing him, no shirt or shoes, just jeans. His smile and how dear he is to me. It's more than I can handle. The answers to these queries and thoughts are beyond my reach. I understand very little of what is happening in me, but have every intention of not pushing myself to the point of insanity. "Time out" is a really good rule and should be exercised often. We can never go back and that has been brought home to me so strongly. Neither can we be the same people we were. I know we have to "go on," as people say, but I can't go on being the person I was before. That person is gone forever. Hopefully a better person may emerge from this confusion, but I will never be the same again.

Already I see that some abilities I used to have are gone forever, but maybe new ones will surface. When you are physically incapacitated, it is so plain to others around you. But when your very being (the self you've always known and depended on) is crushed and your natural way of doing things taken away, leaving you with just a muddle of criss-crossed thoughts to carry you through, I think the only sensible thing to do is go very slowly. I know that with my diminished abilities I am not capable of making very wise decisions, so letting life just happen is my only choice for now. I think Bill is much the same. We tend to just float a little now.

Tuesday, August 24

8:52 I've had my bath and am working toward going to Ark City to have lunch with friends. The raccoon got one chicken and one goose last night. Tonight I'm going to sit out a while to see if I can get him. He sure is eating well. I have my hens shut up in the chicken house so he can't get them. I'll lock the geese up too.

I think of Keith almost constantly, but there are times when he's out of my mind. It's better in some ways now, I don't cry all of the time, either on the inside or the out. The relief from being constantly in pain is such a gift. It's never far, but not as intense. Today I am not going to the cemetery like I did last Tuesday. That was a terrible mistake. Lois said she used to go to Brian's grave often and was able to talk with her son and feel comforted. As much as it bothered me last week, I have a feeling that will not be for me. His grave is a scar on the earth for me. I even hesitate to talk with him in my mind. His torment was so great on this earth I don't want to pull him back to feel the pain again. We all have different ways of grieving and a large part of mine is in trying to let him go. To ask him to share in my pain would be wrong. I somehow have felt the pain that he had here and know what he went through. I carry that as part of my burden but do not resent it. It stops me cold when I start to want him back. That would be very selfish, with no regard for his well-being. I know where he is and that he is safe at last. God's ways are so apparent, if we just look for them. We all know pain and suffering to some degree, but Keith felt them in the extreme.

My limited mind wants to say that losing a child is unnatural, but my realistic mind says that this is not true. All death is natural. Some of us are here for one day, others are here for one hundred years. When we rage, and tell the heavens that a child going before us is unnatural, it is one more exercise in futility.

For example, we can say that it is unnatural for a child to fall, scrape his knee and feel pain, but reality quickly steps in and says, "It's natural that a child sometimes falls and hurts himself." Therefore what we are looking at is just a degree of pain and losing a child is at the top of the scale. There is no true perfection in this world, and even the worst of pain must be felt by some. I am in agreement that, unless you've been there, you can't know what we feel. But, at the same time, we must accept death as just another part of life that is natural.

Someone said to me that some of us have to have more burdens than others. I've probably heard this statement made many times in my life, but it meant nothing until I was forced to carry this one. We tend to think of a burden as almost a weakness on the part of the person who must carry it. We want them to shoulder their load and do it with no complaining. At least that is what I expect of myself. This one is, I'm certain, the worst I'll ever have, and I hope to do it without complaint. I don't want to say, *Lord, Lord, why did you do this to me? I want to say, Lord, I accept your will.* So far, there has been no doubt in my mind as to God's purpose in this and I pray that it stays this way. I worry without conviction and ponder without question. Keith's special ways are allowed to be mine if I don't question. His pain is mine and I own it, but in some ways it's a sweet burden because, like any mother, I would rather carry his pain than have him do it.

Thinking of this as a gift may seem strange to some, but it makes perfect sense to me. It's like when my babies were first born. My back would be aching, my legs would be tired, my eyes would be burning and my arms would be hurting but, as long as that baby was sleeping peacefully in my arms, all was OK. Within minutes after I knew Keith was dead I had the assurance that he was OK and in the arms of God. This doesn't take away my pain but it gives me a peace.

~ ~ ~

My mind evaluates anything and everything first with the question, *Was that before or after?* From that single bit of time when I realized my son was dead there stands a dividing line as strong as the cables that hold up the Golden Gate Bridge. I am forever different from that second on. Whatever innocence was left in me shattered. I will no longer wonder, *What's the worst thing that can happen to me? It has happened.*

In a sense, that is a comfort. I may have to endure this same pain again but I will not be surprised by the magnitude of it. My years left here on earth will have the comfort that nothing ever again will hurt as much as this. Della had to feel this pain three times with three of her children gone and I remember her saying, "*It is not right that we should live beyond our children.*" That stuck in my mind, that she thought not of the one she had just lost but all three of them together. The pain was as one. Losing Bill or any of my other children would be the same, because once you've met the dragon, you don't forget.

~ ~ ~

The carpenters are here mudding the new wallboard. I can see where this might turn into a pretty house yet. I've always been very sensitive to having my surroundings pretty. My personal physical appearance has never been much of a factor to me, but my house being nice is a driving force.

Wednesday, August 25

4:50 Today has been relatively painless. I didn't have to go anywhere and nothing too pressing here to be done, so I've been kind of easy on myself. I've done a lot of little jobs, including a few more thank you notes and letters. They have been a terrible chore to me. My recall on who brought what is zip. I know I've forgotten someone, but the blur of those first days just didn't let me pay attention. I'm so thankful that now I can function day by day. Going from not being able to move from a chair to where I am now seems miraculous. So I can't say there has been no progress.

We have a big raccoon problem. Three geese and about 10 chickens gone. He must be full.

It's still hot! As always I'm looking forward to fall, not to winter though. Since I'm going to be doing a lot of remodeling, maybe this one won't seem so long. Last winter I was snowed and mudded in so much (two 11" snows). Maybe this winter will be easier.

Friday, August 27

2:30 Yesterday I went to Wichita to see Jane, look for carpet and buy groceries. Jane and I ran all over Wichita and it was fun, Janie is always fun. We took Mom to lunch and I think she enjoyed it. I saw Duane and Priscilla too.

Today I've not done a lot, but I was up for a long time last night and I seem to drag around when I don't sleep well. I wrote some letters and have tried to avoid feeling anything. Sometimes it works, and today it did. So much of the time when I do this though I feel like I'm dancing a circle around my inside self. Occasionally I dart in and out of the circle of self. When I am in there where the pain is, I run back out as quickly as I can.

Monday I am going to start on the house again, with all those little jobs: stripping, varnishing, painting and finishing the furniture. This is my next goal.

In a month's time I've gone from struggling to make myself wash the dishes, make my bed and take a bath to being able to leave the house without trembling and tears, to being able to remodel and work on house projects. When I don't think I'm doing well, I think back to where I was just a short time ago. My mind divides my life between the time when Keith was alive and since he has been gone. Maybe that will never end, but perhaps I can become productive again, even with knowing he is gone.

I feel separated from most people by this before-and-after self. Knowing I will never be the same again has become more acceptable. Being a different person now, I will find my way into knowing how this new person wants to live. I don't grow impatient with people who have not felt this kind of pain, but I sure do recognize the shallow ones with a flick of the eye and I have nothing for them. They are so into themselves that they won't miss me anyway. I have no hard feelings or anger, only a nonplussed feeling. Where I thought there were minor friendships there is nothing. This hasn't happened often but just enough for me to notice. I am very surprised at this twist in the cyclone.

6:00   Bill will be home in a few minutes, but I just wanted to jot down a few things that have been going through my mind. I keep thinking about my "before mind" and "after mind." The week before Keith died, I had been quite agitated about how all the trouble would end. I just could not see any good end to what was going on. I knew he was much worse and that his thoughts were only on Doris and the kids. Also he was doing all the wrong things again, not following doctor's orders and self-medicating. He couldn't accept their divorce; I knew that. And I knew that Doris had called the police a number of times. He was totally irrational and had no control of his emotions. He was up against a wall that we all knew would be impossible for him to scale. My mind was constantly on this and I asked Bill a number of times, "How is this going to end?"

I knew he did not have an answer, but I was sensing that something was about to happen. Each day was full of anxiety and worry.

Keith's children were back and forth between here and home in the hopes that we could somehow protect them from the confusion of his bizarre behavior. Only today have I felt strong enough to write about this. The recurrence of his problems seemed to intensify during the time of Wayne's illness and death. Keith had recently lost his job and was trying to create a business of electrical repair. During Wayne's illness he was too often at our house and did anything and everything for Kim. He was so intense about small details that I knew he must be neglecting his own family. After his death, Doris told me that there was never any time that his problems decreased. I am certain she always knew exactly where he was emotionally. But the rest of us began to notice a deterioration after Wayne died. These past two years, the problems escalated. Of course, with it came worry, worry and worry for us. Still, at times in his adult life, we were spared somewhat. Doris never complained, so at times we had on our rose-colored glasses. With this explanation I have tried to explain my "before" thinking. I enjoyed at times believing I had five normal children. But often word of his behavior would filter back into our lives. I remember thinking that maybe when he reached 40 things would change.

Tuesday, Aug. 31

Went to lunch; it was easier today. It seems like there is an allotted number of tears and we are going to cry them, no matter what. Right now I seem to be a little troubled by my lack of concern about my house. It's torn up and dirty and I seem not to care. I look at it and don't see it. I hope I don't stay this way. I've always been a pretty good house-keeper and very diligent. I've always seemed to have a lot of self-motivation, but it has absolutely left me. It just isn't there. The house is torn up from the carpenters, but that dirt at the back door sure wasn't caused by them.

Nothing against the former owner, but there is not one wall or floor or ceiling that is me. If I had to choose one word to describe how it effects me, it would be *depressive*. Maybe when I can start to add colors and designs that appeal to me, I will find care of it more appealing. I do have big intentions, without results.

I've established a routine of getting out of the house, which seems to help somewhat. The hard grief seems to come for shorter periods of time now, but the initial pain from the first second of *knowing* is still alive and well. I don't cry as much, but crying or not crying does not budge it.

Thursday, September 9

Even though I haven't written in a while, I've been writing in my mind. I guess our Keith has been gone for about six weeks. Some of the pain is gone and I've had a few good days, but it always seems as though more is just around the corner waiting for me. I think our defenses go into overtime when needed.

I don't know if it is getting better or if I'm just becoming more adept at running faster. At any rate I've been able to keep myself together for about four or five days.

The carpenter has been here again this week and he is getting close to being done. Then I can go to work.

I'm down to two geese and 15 hens and three roosters. The roosters and hens I'm keeping in the chicken house all the time now. Yesterday I got eggs for the first time, but little eggs.

Bill is feeling better and Friday he will have a lot of dental work. He, of course, thinks he can work Friday with no problem - and he may. He's been on an antibiotic for over a week, so I'm certain his infection is gone. He's already saying he will need cool drinks brought to him on the couch, but in the next breath says he's going to clean out the bottom of the barn, where he fed cows last winter. As usual, it's a "Who knows?"

We had a great time over Labor Day weekend. Billy and Pam put together a competition, with 10 events. I think we had around 30 people here and 19 participated. It was great fun and I'm sure we will do it again next year.

September 15, 1993

Late, and I've accomplished blessed little. It's been awhile, but the carpenters are here, putting the trim around the windows on the new porch, or rather I should say, the new room that started out to be the porch. We've often said "I'd like to have a nickel for every_____". I could probably show a profit if I just had a nickel for every porch we've started that turned into a room. Lest you think I'm a rational, intelligent person, we even put down hardwood flooring that I am now going to carpet.

I woke up at 7:30, had coffee, fed the chickens, helped Bill move cows and fed the cats and dogs. I can't believe the total carnage in this house.

The porch and dining room will be carpeted tomorrow. All the furnishings from those two rooms are now stacked in the kitchen.

Sawdust, sheet rock dust and crumbling black backing from the old carpet now cover the entire house. Do you sense a bit of madness in this house? I love it. Every minute of this chaos is dear to my heart. I can complain and expect sympathy; what more could a wretched soul want!

10:30 Because it's Monday and I am extremely old-fashioned, I've started the laundry. The sidetrack of the hour was cutting strips of cloth for a cro-cheted rug. Age has dictated that I no longer have to be of single purpose but can wander through my days, taking advantage of all distractions. I'm beginning to have a sympathy for my eight-year-old grandson who takes an hour to put on his shoes. His distractions are more numerous than mine.

I welcome the gift of these years of time and mild diversions. The years of being in control of the welfare and whereabouts of five children were satisfying, but a few years between being jailed by total responsibility and the rigors of old age are truly a blessing. If I had assumed any of the monetary responsibilities of this family I probably wouldn't have been able to have these vagabond years.

Do I not remember things to do, or do I sometimes allow encroaching years and old age memory loss to be a convenience? Do you have to know all my secrets!

Let me ask you, is cutting out 2" squares for a quilted piece more important than cutting up green peppers from the garden? The quilt piece will allow beauty for the eye, comfort for the soul and maybe a compliment for the ego. Also, running your hand over a piece that you have quilted yourself is a truly sensual experience. Now, cutting the green peppers to be put in the freezer for later use also has its perks. They will flavor a meatloaf, add taste to an omelet, perk up a smothered steak and be appreciated when I don't have a fresh green pepper. Also I have saved money because the peppers are inexpensive to grow, and I won't pay winter prices for a green pepper. So how do green peppers and 2" squares of fabric weigh against each other? As it's my time and effort, I'll do both. I hope this explains why I'm grateful for the slow middle years. Were I a divorced or widowed woman I would have to work to support myself and these old-fashioned ways and years would be lost to me. Gratitude comes in strange packages sometimes. The shiny, fragrant green peppers are a joy, and the neat, pretty little squares are a pleasure. But the real joy and pleasure come when I realize I've been given a gift in being able to enjoy these things and the greater gift of the time to do it.

Lord knows there is plenty of dirt in this old house I could be pushing around but the rewards are nominal.

Walking Naked

Walking Naked

II

Listening

October 20

I don't remember when I quit writing and am certainly in no shape to go back and read through those writings.

Depression. Right now, that is the name of the game. The salt is not salty, the weather has no significance, rain or shine. Other people's joy and participation in life look peculiar to me. No ups at all, more like a hum. Rather than having the senses jarred by smelling fresh bread or hearing music, my senses are comatose. Throughout my life, because of past depressions, I've trained myself to find happiness and joy in a child's smile or the fine smell of a clear, running creek. Now I am just mechanical. I have a list of "Things I Do":

1. Go to lunch with the girls on Tuesday
2. Go to club (friends)
3. Work on remodeling every day
4. Try to keep myself groomed
5. Eat

Today the wind is howling and is so desolate that it goes with the dryness of my soul. Did God lose this battle? Do you have my son or don't you? Did the darkness and lack of hope win out and take him someplace to be tortured forever? You ask me, with no reservations, to hope and believe in you. Then why in hell won't you answer me? I know I'm pushing the issue, but with this kind of pain, I feel pushy. I feel entitled to know the answer. Kneeling at the side of his grave with no relief at all is just not fair.

You are supposedly the one who loves us so much and I think I at least deserve an answer to this question! Is this the bargaining stage of grief, or the anger part? Being dry and angry at the same time is a big load.

November 9

Some of the anger is going and some letting go of Keith is happening. God puts the fierceness of a thousand armies in our soul when he gives us a child. When he allows one of them to be taken from us, Oh, my! the windmills we fight. We make Don Quixote look like a puff ball. We mothers could challenge and defeat great armies in defense of our children. But when death is the enemy and no matter our anger, we still lose. Our rage is as though the world were blown apart, but it's all inside us. No amount of wrath at God will bring Keith back to me. I have to give him to God for safekeeping, and no mother (at least one like me) gives her child to anyone else without a fight to the bitter end.

The other day I spoke with Mary. I said a rosary for Keith and it fell on Tuesday, so it was the Sorrowful Mysteries. Needless to say, it was overpowering. I have found a new Mary that I didn't know before and I know she is on my side. At least I know she understands this sorrow.

I am now working on getting some conversation going with God. At present it is more sparring than communicating. I pray for Keith and give a little of him to God each time. I can't give all of him to God at once, so I do it in a miserly way. Small bits, only as much as I can.

It's more like, "If you insist upon having him, please do your job well." That may sound harsh, but at least I'm not screaming at him, saying "*Can't you do anything right?*" Surrender comes hard and slow.

We went to Branson over the weekend and met friends there. We went to shows and ate nonstop. Prime rib twice. Saw the Baldknobbers, Roy Clark and Yakov Smirnoff. It was fun and the diversion, as always, was soothing to the soul.

Am taking a grandson to the doctor in Ponca City for headaches today, so I will go to the store and run a few errands there.

November 11

God seems to be trying to get me to realize something, and I seem to be getting a message. I will state plainly what this message seems to be: That God allowed Keith to be taken shows me how much He loves me. This, according to my rational mind, is TOTAL lunacy, but somehow my heart says to listen. Only by being defeated and destroyed can I begin to understand God's way. If I look at this strictly from the standpoint of God's relationship to Keith, it is simple to see why He would allow Keith to be let out of his suffering. But this destruction of my very being is so hard to understand. Only by being crushed and having to extend my hand to His Mother have I begun to understand a little bit.

My relationship with Mary was always secondary. I just couldn't get what the big deal was and I questioned seriously why I couldn't acquire any closeness with her. Now I can understand how she suffered and her patience and obedience. She opened herself up totally to me. Her revelation of herself to me has been acted out in such a simple way. It's as though I've always known her most intimately. Her persuasion with her son is so profound. I know this because I know Keith does not want me to suffer. I should feel nothing but joy at where he is, and it is only my frailties that prevent me from this happiness. I know I have not explained clearly why I know that God loves me so much He took my son. I will pray that He gives me clarity in understanding His way. My praying the rosary for Keith has been my first real comfort in a long time. I know that only in this place can I find the truth.

We are always and constantly under a bombardment of information (revelation) from God. He reveals Himself to us, but we are often blind to what He shows us. Reading about another person's opinion or experience (eg., self help, personal gain, psychology, religious or spiritual books, etc.), I have come to believe that God at times speaks to us through other people. Some have the gift of listening and the gift of interpretation. Our responsibility in this plan is discernment. All are gifts of the spirit and should be used wisely.

Were this not so, we would gain nothing from one another. Without discernment we would only be "as the gong," and all language would be but a babble. That we read and, in turn, experience the gifts and wisdom of another I consider a "perk." If I had only my mind, my experience, my education and curiosity to listen to, I would still be crawling on the ground and wearing a diaper.

III

Reality

Walking Naked

January 8

Billy's birthday tomorrow. Made it through Christmas with lots of pain, and I treated the whole season with a brutal, to the point, let's-get-this-done-and-over-with attitude. Someday I'm sure I will again feel mellow toward the holidays instead of being like a "woman with a mission."

~ ~ ~

Helen (Billy's dog) is in labor on the couch; Grandma is reading her Christmas cards again. Mom is living here with us. It became apparent to us that she could not live alone any longer. Her mind is closed to any input, only "output" comes from it. Confusion reins.

Bill and Loren have gone to town to get a paper. Loren is here because he has been such a poop at home. The biggest problem is that he's smarter than all of us and puts us through the hoops. It will all work out.

Wayne's stone has been placed at his grave in the cemetery. It is made of limestone and is the same height he was, 6'6". Standing next to it, I feel as though I am standing next to him. I can't say exactly what I feel when I stand there, but I feel a strength and comfort when I do.

These last months are a blur and I suppose will remain that way. That Keith is truly gone from us has made its painful way into my heart. It's such an awful truth that it can only become real to me in little bits. The whole truth at once would not be bearable. My soul is malignant with what I know already. It grows slowly and robs me every day of joy. But somewhere, somehow, God lays a support under me and gives me times when I almost forget Keith is gone.

Person Keith Hess

He was the baby, young child, little boy, young man and adult who never grew emotionally, never satisfied or fulfilled, never gratified at a job well done. No gift or pleasure given to him was enough to fill the hunger that tormented him.

I suppose he could have been termed "genius level" in intelligence and "totally deprived" emotionally. To me his mind was a clear, crisp, efficient entity that saw far beyond what I am capable of seeing. It was like an exercise trail with stopping places and signs that give you instructions on calisthenics to do. His mind stopped at each opportunity to clarify a problem, like a perfect body that was able to perform exacting exercises. His more-than-average intellect solved and understood each knowledge opportunity. But, when even the most simple act demanded a basic emotional understanding, he was as helpless as an infant. This is not to say he was not capable of love, because he loved with an intensity that had no boundaries. I never saw an indifferent or casual side to his caring. His love for his wife and children was like a runaway train, full of power and force but with no control.

His torment had a life of its own that never let up in its pursuit of him. No counselor or pill or alcohol could penetrate that blank, mindless space that was his self-control center. It was as if he was made like a clock with a defective hour hand. The minute hand worked with an efficiency that amazed all who knew him. But with an hour hand whirring out of control there was no success and, most often, fanatical confusion.

I always knew Keith loved me, and the pain and worry he caused were not purposefully thought-out. Also, I was never afraid of him. These are two gifts I cherish.

I was totally unprepared and uneducated to deal with a child like Keith. With the other four, all I had to do was to care for, love and teach. They learned and flourished. With Keith it was a running battle from day one.

When someone cannot learn, and then respond to what is being taught, there is immense frustration.

My perseverance never wavered and his ability never improved. In some ways I thank God that I never gave up and in other ways I know my ineptitude caused some harm. With each crisis I had hope that he would learn, but he didn't. It never occurred to me to seek counseling for us. My scope wasn't developed that far, back then. My drive was to raise him and, in my ignorance, I know I caused harm. I had always felt guilty about this until after he died, when the guilt reached a peak that had to be dealt with. I did a thorough examination of my conscience and asked myself, "Did I mean to do harm to Keith with this error?" Each error I could remember came back with the answer, "I did the best I knew how with what I knew." There were only two times when I knew I was out of control and did harm. I took those to God and begged his forgiveness. Those memories are dimmer now, barely remembered. If God can forgive me, I must be generous and forgive myself.

I know it seems that I am dwelling on the negative and maybe I am. The most predominant parts of Keith's life were negative. But without the embarrassment, would I have learned the humility? Without the frustration, would I have known how to persevere? Without the guilt, would I have learned to forgive myself? This list could go on for a long time, but it says to me that possibly what Keith did not possess, I had to learn. And even the negative had value.

He died in a poverty of mind and spirit that caused even the most hard-hearted to stop and mourn a little. He was well-liked by all he touched, and his funeral sprouted a variety of people that looked like a bouquet of flowers picked from the finest gardens to the lowest pasture weed. Both the junkie and the judge came to say good-bye to him, and all those in between.

I feel justified in my sorrow and also in my joy that his pain is over. My regrets are few and my thankfulness is huge. Among average people, we feel comfortable and safe, but to know the gifted and the deprived gives us wealth.

Dear Reader,

During the months of January or February, 1994, I attended a weekly grief group in Wichita, 80 miles from here. The group met on Tuesday nights for about nine weeks. Somewhere in this time we wrote letters to and from Grief, which has its own identity. It lives and breathes its own life. Writing to it, and its writing to me, was as natural to me as calling a friend for a chat on the phone. I was me and it was itself at that time. Somewhere during those comatose months of not living, not writing, not participating, I came to not fear grief. I accepted it as a part of my life, for that time in my life.

Dear Grief:

The heat of a volcano seems to be warm water compared to your searing. The wind of a hurricane is a mild breeze compared to the trashing you cause to a soul. A breaking dam of water is a mild touch compared to the powerful weight you exert to suppress living. I think only a howl from the depths of hell could exceed your power.

You are my enemy. I must endure your tortures and turn them into a victory. My suffering must be turned into the most exquisite rose, with the scent of Keith's neck as I inhaled it when he was a baby. Only then can I lay it at the feet of Christ as a perfect gift.

I have always known that losing a child would be the ultimate that a human would be asked to endure. It is true. Losing one child seems equal to losing all your children. I know now the deficiency of human language. No artist can paint it. No singer of songs can wail it. It cannot be captured by our human abilities. It can't stand before us to be looked at and understood.

In this we are blessed and the only answer is, "Thank you, Father."

Sylvia Hess

P.S. Grief, your victory is as empty as the one who sent you. Would I have ever kissed the feet of

Christ on the cross without you to show me His suffering? Would Mary ever have made herself so available to me as she has in the Sorrowful Mysteries? Would the mercy of Jesus ever have covered me without you? Sometimes I wonder why you just don't give up. The enemy did not win my son. From outward appearances it might seem that you won, but I know the truth.

Grief to Me

Dear One:

I know you hate me and want me to go away forever, but I need to explain myself to you before I can go away.

One of the things you have noticed is that I scramble your mind like a bowl of eggs about to go into the skillet. There are a number of reasons for this. In your racing mind that is full to capacity, I'm lending a slowing process to keep you from throwing yourself into despair, which would cripple you to any further joy in your life.

I've slowed your step some, to keep you from hurting your body. I don't mind that you work at a steady pace, but I don't want you to hurry and harm yourself. I know you are used to running to each job you do, but with this added burden you need to slow down a bit.

I don't let you sleep at times because I want you to have that quiet, awake, nothing-can-be-done-now-anyway time. You feel your hurts more at this time but it's far more beneficial to feel them than it is to stuff them somewhere like the ironing you don't want to finish now. Like the ironing, the pain doesn't get done stuffing it somewhere while you do something else with your time.

Please, don't dislike me for these "I could be sleeping" times. Just turn up the furnace, get comfortable and abide with me.

I know I bring you pain by way of indifferent, pushy and insensitive people, blind acquaintances and boring professionals. Hey! Just look at this as the time to practice perfect humility.

Oh, I forgot when I was talking about time, that I often, while giving you sleeplessness, don't give you enough working time. I know it seems these are opposing, but hey, you would suffer more if you weren't pushed and kept busy.

I put you off into la la land when ordinarily you would be listening to what someone was saying but at the same time I give you a keenness to hear what you should be hearing.

I give you a sweet realization of the extreme value of life and, at the same time, knowledge that the greater the value of the loss, the more painful it is. This can also allow you to unite with Christ's suffering on the cross.

I know my ways bring about a great loneliness and isolation, and you feel removed from any human comfort. You are not going to like this, but it will eventually give you acceptance. Finally you will come to accept this as a mystery. How many times have you railed at that answer? But truly it will give you a finely honed humility that humans need so much.

I will corrupt your joy and sometimes cloud what should be happy times. I think this will teach you that the realities of this life are both joy and sorrow.

I will teach you to be more lenient and less judgmental. I will crush the hardened heart and make it weep. I will turn your eyes from this world to the next. I will plunge you into the darkest of the dark, the blackest of the black, but soon the light will come. Not so you will forget the dark, but so you will appreciate the light. I will wrench you, torment you, haunt you, suffocate you, bewilder you, tear away at your soul, cause friction, hardship and misery. I will create chaos, confusion and guilt. I will force you to deeply examine yourself, to question if you've ever done anything right. I will put you to the test. But, if I have done my job, you will endure pain, not be so frightened, see your world with more clarity, perfect your soul, mend hurts, expect less and look for good. I will clear your mind for the best of this world and show you what you've done right. You will certainly have passed the test. God will have shown you your strength and your weaknesses if you look to him.

I am a teacher of the finest quality, if you want to learn.

I am,
Grief

~ ~ ~

I could say volumes more on this and there are more tears to fall, but today took care of today and tomorrow will take care of tomorrow.

I have felt and know Keith's pain. It is as real to me as if I had suffered it. I know the deep sadness it creates in me. Now it brings to me a great need to exert mercy. Mercy to everyone I meet, know, or love. You, on your cross, knew the pain of each and every human that has ever or will ever live. This gives me full and sure knowledge that your mercy to us has no limitations.

Even if you were not divine and you did not use your divinity, we would have to be always in awe of the fact that you foretold and completed the act of hanging on the cross. Using only the tools of a human you accomplished what no other human could.

With only Keith's suffering as a guide, I have been given a glimpse of your suffering. This has made me more aware of how much sin pains you. As much as sin causes you pain, our indifference to you must be even more painful. Strange to say, but I am grateful that past sins in my life, particularly sins of omission, were committed knowing of your disapproval. Without that knowledge I would have remained indifferent to them and never have been able to rectify them. This is a comfort to me now. My youth said, *"My will and no one else's,"* and certainly not *"Your will."* I didn't even know about your will. Yet I knew I was missing something very important. I know now I wanted peace, but had no idea how to get it.

Later on I figured out that doing for others gave me a great joy and satisfaction. I should be saying that these gifts all came from you. You have let me grow in you and at the same time allowed me to think that I had some part in it.

With Keith's death you have given me a compassion that was never in me before. I feel the pain of others most acutely. Also a few times you have put people before me who complain adamantly about the very thing they should be thanking you for, each and every day. Suffering comes before me like a real object, it has form and truth to it.

The amazing truth is that if we suffer under God's will, the mercy is of such abundance that we are unable to find fault with the suffering and come to understand its purpose.

Grief and Spirituality

This pairing comes from letting my grief happen, which is rather alien to me. First, let me explain this to you. Having gone through periods of depression, I've realized that the reality of happiness is a decision. When I figured out that the responsibility for my happiness was my very own business, I began to practice seeing the good in most everything and pitching the bad to the side. Being a person of physical and environmental depression made this a very challenging but rewarding decision process.

Having trained myself in this way, it is difficult for me to let the sorrow and the sadness have their way. So back to pairing the grief and spirituality. For me it feels unnatural that the two meld together, even though this union came directly from God in the form of His divine mercy. I have not been angry with God for taking Keith to His merciful heart. However, I once threw a temper tantrum and yelled at Him.

For a long time my grief and spirit were not traveling on the same highway. Grief was on Route 1 and spirit was on Route 2, traveling parallel at about the same speed. Slowly the distance between the roads narrowed and moved toward an eventual joining. I wanted to keep them separate because I found my faith to be a comfort and the sorrow to be a negative. I fought hard to bring positive thought and action into my life and didn't want to join sorrow and faith together.

Along the spirit road God was, in His mercy, filling my mind and heart with truth, knowledge and understanding. There were many things He needed to teach me before I could combine both the grief and spirit into one. He taught that having less was more. He gave me a sureness and certainty that finished my total acceptance of His divinity. Much like a gift that has been carefully carried home from the store and wrapped in a most neat and caring way, so was my faith. But looking at this wrapped box, it was apparent that the bow had not been placed to complete its specialness. The bow was a union formed by Keith's, my own and Jesus Christ's suffering. Just like water is water, heat is heat and air is air, suffering is suffering. Like water, heat and air there are varying degrees of suffering.

Keith was put to his limit, I was put to mine and Jesus suffered all. There lies Christ's divinity and our union with Him.

Seeing a crucifix now yanks me to attention, where before it was only a symbol of my faith. Now it is truly alive with Christ's suffering. The Stations of the Cross were just a story, now they are alive with reality. A rosary isn't just a prayer. My heart aches for Our Lady and is in awe of her strength. The religious calendar on my wall isn't just a hint of who I am, but a proclamation. The crown of thorns is not a picture, but painted and glistening with the sharpness of steel, driven with total accuracy. Those weren't brittle thorns that could be snapped between our fingers but were hard, destined and piercing missiles. Each one would be far more than we could endure, but He embraced them all for us. He didn't take his divinity to the cross like a pain pill to be taken when it got too rough, but stayed with us in our suffering to endure it all. Isn't it just more than we can grasp?

So, in our grief, we are not pleading to someone who looks at us as though He doesn't quite know why we are so upset and can't just "buck up and go on." We are communicating with the "gold medalist" of suffering. The winner of winners. He "owns" suffering, plus He has the ability to relieve ours.

I knew from the first, within minutes, that I could not endure this pain. After the phone call, I went out to the back step and began to die.

I have survived some of the sin and suffering that this world has to offer. Each one took it's pound of flesh and went on its way. This one was the ultimate and I could not survive it. I stood there, looked up at the night and began to die. My heart was ceasing to beat, my whole being - body and soul - was leaving this earth.

I reached up to God and from the depths of my soul I cried to Him saying, "I can't do this!" knowing that in an instant I would be gone. Instead I was swept up, the sweep covering each fiber of my body with healing and my soul surrounded by a firm strength. It could be described as being scooped out of a stormy sea by a helicopter rescue, being put aloft by wind force or lifted by the talons of an eagle and saved, then a hand supported me and broke my fall.

In the next instant I was afloat, suspended and secured by real force, like floating on water, maybe. And then stood back gently on my feet. Then I knew I would not only live, but be cradled by my father. Whatever was to come, I would make it through.

Christ's mercy came to me in an instant. No, that is not correct. There was no time involved; no time passed. It just was. I turned and went in to tell Bill that Keith was dead.

Our Lord kept me here to teach me, to purify my convictions.

I am inaccessible in many ways. The location of my home and my demeanor say "Don't get too close." I have made myself a recluse and this time has become a filled vessel. All these things did not happen by accident but have served the purpose of making me receptive to be taught. Again and again, "There is a reason for everything." Often times I am given the impression and knowledge that Keith's death served multiple purposes: to end his suffering, to save my soul . . .

There is a distinct pattern to my learning. It is consistent, yet periodic. It comes with a clarity that demands acceptance. But first my wall of defense against the pain of this world had to be shattered. Unbroken, I would not have been vulnerable to learning. The bricks had been laid and mortared around my heart.

I did not suffer much, feel much, or have an open view of the pain of others. Now that enclosure has been broken and swept away. I suffer, I feel and know the pain of others now. False pain in others is glaring to me now and I have no time for it. I think when a grieving person says, "My priorities have changed" we don't mean *I would have done it differently or I love my children or husband or friends more.* I think we mean we are more vulnerable to you, we are enlightened to the goodness in you, your truth is more apparent to us. I'm not presuming what others might feel, but suffering is universal, I believe, in it's teaching. Along with this new awareness, comes a perception of false pain that is keen.

Now a walk behind a wheelchair doesn't fill me with frustration at the slowness or discomfort at the infirmity but with a true gratitude for my legs and an empathy for the person. When I match my pace with their steps they don't seem as slow as they used to. Listening to the jumbled speech of a person with dementia, it sounds much more important and gift-filled than it ever has before.

I am not saying that because I suffered I have found the secret of being a better person than you are; I am just saying it has made a difference in me. But these gifts only come if we are open to them. God didn't jump in and say, "OK, Toots, move over, I'll take care of this." He is so polite and will stand by patiently waiting, until we issue an invitation (or knock).

I believe I could have taken the way of hatred, anger and self-pity, but in my vulnerability and self preservation I opted for his mercy.

There are many tears left to be shed, hurts to be felt, guilt to heal and forks in the road. But with guidance, I well search for the way of hope. Psalm: 86 1-7, 11-12.

IV

Hope

Walking Naked

.

May 25, 1995

8:00 Early today I was the old woman walking up the long drive to the mailbox, moaning because her legs ached, only it was my heart. But this evening, as I was cooking, and my two youngest children (ages 31 and 32) were out playing, I thought to myself that the past times when I was cooking and the kids were out playing were the sweetest of memories. Later, as this woman walked up the long drive pushing a beautiful nine-month-old grandson in his stroller, Oh! how much happier the heart. Each day is a lifetime, it seems, and each lifetime a day.

May 26

Up at 7:00 with Dalton Do, he was ready, right now, to take on the world. Bill and I followed much later with two pots of coffee. Jane on the move to shower, feed Dalton, mix milk etc., etc., etc.

Double batch of chocolate chip cookies and french toast, and loving every minute of it. Why not, with some of my very most favorite people here with me?

The Annual, 15th Year

When our youngest son Billy was a junior in high school, on Memorial Day they had their first "Annual." It was a camp-out on a lake 30 miles south and east of home. My recollections of the first two years are of Bill and me driving down on the Saturday or Sunday afternoon to do what we had done all their lives: go watch whatever our kids were doing. They probably numbered around 150 to 200 people, having a great time together. From the heart, the blessing I feel is that Billy didn't wait till we're not around to have fun. The "Annual" has continued to be a yearly event, hence it's title.

As of the day before yesterday, a little city has been forming down in the pasture that is the closest to the creek. We are the hosts this year to the Annual. It's early in the festivities and the pastures are not all torn up yet, so I am still grateful that we get to do this. But please check back with me Tuesday morning.

Friday, May 26, 1995

4:00   I made a very stupid statement the other day in the form of a question: "What stigma?" And, worse yet, I was in a room with about 10 other suicide survivors! How could I have forgotten the fear? Also, how could I have forgotten that some people in my world thought Keith's death was insignificant? People like Keith, who are down and out when they die, are sometimes looked at as something to be swept off the porch. The porch is a little cleaner and looks better, so the world is better off. Also some even thought that our life would be better, and someone even said to me, "Don't you really feel a little relieved?" I wanted to scream at them, "Do you think my life is better because my son is buried?" But always I have to think they just don't know any better. And right after that the thought comes, "Thank God."

Pity is a poor substitute for respect. His life was so precious to me.

Well, anyway, I'm feeling like my hide is being hung out to dry again and the sun is relentless.

One of the campers called to tell the others he is broken down west of town and they are all off to the rescue. Dalton is taking a nap, the sun just came out, it's quiet and I know that for this moment I'm safe. But as we all know, babies sleep fast. Soon there will be enough ruckus around here to chase away the boogie man (grief) again.

~ ~ ~

Grief doesn't quit just because it's two years old. It does let you begin to live again and it even lets you forget for a while, but it is ever faithful and returns to the nest.

The other day I spoke with a couple who are a year down the road from their daughter's suicide. We were talking about what parts of a 24-hour period that our thoughts are free of pain. They are right at the three-minute mark and I realized I am now at about 50-50, so I've covered alot of ground in the second year.

The first two days of the Annual are sort of a setup, pre-event. The campfire crowd on Wednesday and Thursday night is pretty much men only. I went for a beer at 10:00 each night, and it was a little rough for me. But if you are going to "belly up to the bar" you surely know you aren't here for a tea party. Friday campfire is a "dress rehearsal" for Saturday night's big event. It's been pretty well established who will be in attendance and each player is in place. The main event is certainly on Saturday night.

One of the man-boy games they play is called the "Duct Taping." All know that, if they are not on guard, they could be the target of this ritual. When someone falls asleep, he is taped to his lawn chair, then netted and subjected to all sorts of ego insult. No one is harmed physically but the personal insult is extreme and photos are taken that will remind him of his sleepy folly forevermore.

Mornings at camp are not sacred at all. You will be wakened to fully enjoy the harm you've done to yourself the previous night. Daytime naps are allowed and not disturbed. The creek attracts some in the daytime and various chores are done or errands ran.

But, all in all, it's a work-up for the Saturday night campfire. I think I can best describe it in this way:

"The Handshake"

I've seen men's handshakes mean a lot of things, mutual victory, introduction, congratulations. Express admiration, seal contracts and indicate agreement. I've seen it say "I know you don't think I should be here, but I'll be civil if you will." The list could go on and on. Last night I witnessed a type of handshake I've never seen before. I'm sure many have, but this time I was the privileged one. It was among six to eight men around the campfire at Saturday night's annual gathering.

There were about 30 to 40 people there. The fire was enormous, taller than I am. It was just after dark, supper was over, children were on moms' laps or just not far away. The breeze was turning a little cool and some reached for sweatshirts or long pants. But it was a nice campfire, some wind, and starry skies, a clear night. Two guitars were played with accomplished ease and the voices of the guitarists sang favorites of their own and others.

Between these charter member of "The Annual" I began to see an occasional handshake. These were interspersed with laughter and man-type insults. But as I began to really pay attention, I noticed an intention to the men's purposeful meandering. Each one paused beside or before another and offered his hand, with true affection and often with spoken words. But more often than not, the handshake stood alone. It made me think of the Vietnam memorial statue of the soldiers frozen in action. This handshake said "I'm grateful for you and the year that allowed us to be here again. In my own way I pray for you in the next year to come. And, most of all, I'm so grateful that you are here right now." There was a promise to it that said, "If you are ever in trouble, please call me first." It said, "Your sorrows affect me and your joys are mine." I'm sure that it said a million other things, known only to them and that the contract is resealed year after year.

I feel very privileged to have witnessed this and thankful for their goodness. I know that if my boy needs help in any way, it would take no more than a phone call to bring the strength of brave lions to his side. This true affection and love (they would hoot at the words) for one another is generous and of the truest sort.

Again I'll say I am grateful for seeing this. But, more than that, I am truly grateful for the handshake that tells it all.

Sunday of "The Annual"

I don't really know what happened Sunday, it just happened. I do know I overslept, missed Mass and now have to go to confession. But what a sweet obligation! I cooked a big breakfast for the two grandsons who had stayed all night and who had eaten S'mores and potato chips for dinner the night before. I did my daily housework, wrote awhile and escaped to the creek with grandson Terry. Later I managed to throw together a ham and macaroni casserole. Camp was slow, calm and, in general, sort of placid. A good day for the kids and the adults as well.

Monday, May 29, 1995

Camp this morning was as dull as it ever gets. No enthusiasm to break camp. Some were doggedly working, some were still asleep, some just sat still at the fire and stared into nowhere.

My visit to the campsite was short. The grandsons were there, one asleep and one with a new-found friend. I brought the latter two up and fed them. They were soon off to investigate a dead chicken in the ravine.

My enjoyment of the Saturday night campfire allowed me to forget to shut the chicken house door.I figure if all the damage we had was one dead chicken we were in good shape.

A little later, when Doris came for the boys, we visited and had breakfast. Soon after, Bill and I were sent a message to come to camp. We went and I'm not sure exactly what happened but it was another little ritual that is called "The icing of the Bull." It came in liquid form, was passed around with a lot of old "war stories" being told about past annuals.

After a few passings of refreshment, I went to the house for a nap. If you really need to understand more about this ritual, you'll just have to drop by next year. I do have four extra beds upstairs.

After I woke and looked at the clock that said 4:30 pm, I wondered where the day went. Bill and I had a hamburger, played backgammon and wandered back outside to go check on a cow that is ready to calve and to bring the others all back to the east pastures. As we passed camp, there were a few guys left who assured me they were telling the total truth to one another. We decided that maybe the grandson who was still there should come to the house and ride into town in the morning with Bill. I went to my garden and spent a pleasurable time there. My grandson came up and asked a question typical of a child who has just had the time of his life: "What are we going to do now?"

As I looked up into his face I realized that soon would come a time when "going to Grandma's" would be last on his list, but my heart begs for him to come occasionally to give it a good warming up.

I added insult to injury by answering his question, "Nothing." So he helped me by hauling some dirt and digging a trench for a railroad tie and various other little chores. Around 7 p.m. I heard the last of the campers pull out. Bill came by and rescued us both by finishing the trench and putting in the tie. Bill makes even the least of chores so much fun. We came in, had ice cream and played around with old nursery rhymes. Bill would tell his version, which was a little colorful, I struggled to remember the real words and our grandson laughed at Grandpa. We turned out all the lights, lit a lamp and tried to imagine what it was like back when there was no electricity. I looked up and it was 10 p.m. so I announced I was going to bed. Bill took his shower and read a little bit and the grandson watched an old Western on TV. Anyway, I went to bed a fully content woman and slept like a baby.

~ ~ ~

Tuesday, May 30

I want to write but must feed the dogs, cat and chickens first.

Chores done, Buck Dog is eyeing the chickens, Ginger Dog is eyeing Buck's food and telling me that dry cat food is not going to cut it. They don't understand that "Monday morning" (although it's Tuesday, because of Labor Day) comes, even down on the ranch.

Everyone is gone and I can't help but compare it to that horrible Monday almost two years ago when everyone had left on Sunday and Bill went back to work. As it was then, the house has been full for a number of days. Of course, these days were a fun time and, as always when any of the kids are here, my heart fills to capacity. The alone days here are fine with me but I kind of feel as though they are like the gathering of ingredients for a recipe. Being productive is a gift beyond measure and I enjoy working, but the frosting comes from family or friends sharing the fruits of our labors. I can then find joy in being able to go to the cellar and bring up a jar of jelly.

I've gotten a little off track here with what I want to say.

This Annual weekend (that lasted six days), in comparison to last year on Memorial Day weekend, is like comparing cow manure to a fine perfume. (Bill would disagree, as he thinks the barnyard smell is a fine aroma.) Last year, as I walked through the grocery store, drug store, variety store and just about anywhere I went, the wreaths and crosses filled with flowers first seemed to assault and then suffocate me. My heart still ached and was in shreds. For many months I had been in limbo, able to function in the everyday world, but still so wounded. My movements through life were robotic and all my feelings were still in a box that was marked "Grief" on the outside.

Something wonderful happened to me this weekend. I found myself saying a little prayer that went something like this, "Lord, please let me live until the next annual." I realized this is the first time I've wanted to live long enough to look forward, instead of living in a vacuum. I have never been suicidal through this time but where the good Lord had me, "here" or "there", was of no concern to me. I remember thinking, *It really doesn't matter, because there are just about as many people in heaven that I love as there are here*. My heart still yearns to see my boy, but my soul wants to stay. My life is forever changed and the tears and pain are still alive and well, but it is with great gratitude that I've realized I want to - and look forward to - living out the rest of my time here. I know that this means saying good-bye to him for a while and it's the saddest of good-byes. My heart is breaking.

I can't write any more now.

A Favorite Keith Story

When Keith was about 11 or 12, he fell in love, hard love. I think he gathered up all the information he knew about this sort of thing, purchased a box of candy and proceeded to this cute little girl's house. We were living in the country then, too, and it seems like it was within walking distance. We knew the girl's family, and later her mom related the event back to me. As I recall, the candy was held behind the back and her dad was taken aback as he answered the door to what was, I'm sure, the first of the predators to march up that path.

In our home, after about a week and a half of various endeavors, maybe an encounter and a little strange behavior, Keith came to me and he said, "Mom, I've decided that I don't like being in love. It makes my stomach hurt and everything." I guess maybe at the end his stomach may have got to hurting just too much.

Another Story

One time when our oldest son had been home for a visit and was leaving for California out of Wichita, we went up early and had lunch with some of the other kids. We were ordering and I was feeling a little frisky and let them order a "Long Island Iced Tea" for me. This is the most innocent tasting drink I ever drank, goes down like liquid gold and puts a glow to the day - complete with a rainbow. After lunch they poured me into the back seat of the car and off we went to the airport. As Glenn got his luggage and said good-bye, I just, from the car, said a non-teary good-bye and smiled through it all. Since then, I've heard comments that the only way Mom should go to the airport is with a snootful of iced tea.

June 1, 1995

Today I sit here and realize how very thankful I am that I survived the first few months - and even the two years after Keith's death. Thankful that I survived those first few hours when I felt trashed like a piece of garbage in the dump outside of town, only I had been dumped just outside of the living. I've heard the term "walking death" and I accept that with one reservation: I wasn't able to walk. My mind was tightly twisted like a rope, burnt at both ends, of little use to anyone. The only emotion other than pain that I had left was gratitude for home and the people I loved. The healing has been slow, slow, slow. At some point I had to accept that this pain would never go away, but that it would lessen. I just wanted it to go away, even for one moment.

It has.

First it was five minutes and eventually I've come to have long periods of peace. I own them, I earned them and I claim them. The pain comes back to visit and rushes through me like sweeping fire but it's not as cruel as it was and never outstays its allotted time. It's been my teacher, a very stern one. I know it will come again but I'm confident it has lost its power to totally crush me. I am a survivor.

I looked at the calendar this morning and realized it was June 1st. The fact that I will have to face what would have been Keith's 38th birthday on the 30th of June hit me hard. Not with the force it did last year, but still with a sting on my heart. This June I won't be dragged through the month like something caught on the back of a pickup truck, only to be left beside the road. Next month will be the two-year anniversary of his death, the 4th of July will pass by without his presence and, before I can turn around, the winter holidays. I know I will pause many times on all these days and other times, but again and again I know the pain will be less and less.

"Miss it, he was my pain."

After mulling this over for a while I figured it out. In the last two or three months I've often felt the lack of pain when I thought about Keith and missed the pain and almost tried to reconstruct it - almost, but not quite. Then with a shake of the brain my Kansas, no-nonsense self corrects my course of thought with, *Are you crazy! Why would you want that pain back?* So I've stuffed it in the don't-think-that-way box and gone on.

When I reread that "Miss it, he was my pain" statement, I began to realize that the pain I was trying to hold onto was really my love for Keith. That pain was the last closeness I had to him and this Mama Bear didn't want to give it up.

We might want to be a little less critical of the widow who, long after we judge she should be getting over her loss, still mourns so deeply. Also, please spread a wide path of understanding for the mom or dad who has lost a child and, years later, still doesn't handle some situations the way we feel they should. There's really no problem with them, it's just a longing that doesn't ever seem to go away. Cradle their heart with a gentle touch on their arm and let yourself share in their memories. It won't take much time and they will recover quickly. Don't judge or panic, just relax and for that brief time be your brother's keeper.

An open letter to priests:

"Know that I love you and am with you always."
Our Lord said this, and so should we.

Think back to the bedside visits you have made, to those most ill you ever stood by. Remember the most suffering cancer patient you have been with, to help them tolerate unendurable pain. Gather together all that you recall, make them into a bundle of one, and you might come near the disabling pain felt by a mother who has lost her child by suicide.

My son died on Monday night, and the funeral was on Thursday. Until the next Monday, I was in shock. I had withdrawn into a cocoon that was filled with the sweet comfort of a combination of drugs and shock. I couldn't see or hear much of anything. It was as if I had been set on cruise control, but I couldn't hear the sound of the engine or the wind. Pain killer and silence filled the air of the cocoon. There was no window or door to this cocoon, no messages came in or out. I believe, had you been standing beside me, you would have been near the most ill person you ever ministered to. You were not there. Were you aware of my situation? Technically, yes. But, had you been fully aware of my great need, you would have hurried to be with me and my family.

On Monday the cocoon lost its comfort. It shattered into a million pieces and, as it did, it pierced my very being. No part of me was left untouched. Grief raged and roared its way into me as nothing else ever had. I had taken no more pills, and shock evaporated into the outside air. The fullness of grief's power had found its target. From that day until three months later, I could not even pass by my church - let alone go into it - without floods of pain and tears. Knowing I would cause a ruckus if I went, I stayed away from Mass.

I live in a town that has no church, so I went to three different nearby churches, all within a 35-minute drive. So to say that any one priest of these churches should have been here is not my point. I understand my lack of planting roots by not attending one of these churches regularly may have allowed each of them to think another one was attending to our needs. Any priest would have been gratefully welcomed. None called. None came. The point I'm trying to make is this: you are more needed than you obviously are aware of. We have survived your obvious lack of awareness of our need for your presence. I am trying to hold no grudge, but have felt the harm. I am writing this, in part, so that others won't have to feel the pain of your absence.

Know that if you feel that ministering to the ill is part of your commitment, you'll never find anyone in greater need than those left behind after a suicide.

My purpose here is to plead for your attention. I know you are overworked and often weary with the load. I know that you may be uncomfortable and question your role in this type of situation. And it might seem that more than enough care is being given to the afflicted. But here you must look hard at your own duty and what you represent.

I know that no one can bail out of the allotted pain, but you do represent another element in the life of the survivors. If I needed guidance in my faith I wouldn't call my plumber to ask his advice. I wouldn't call my dentist to hold my hand and to share this pain. Most especially I would not call the pharmacist to bring the body of Christ to my soul. This entreaty is directed to the priesthood: If a mother who has lost a child is not standing before you at Mass to receive communion, stop and listen for her call. You will never find a home-bound person, that you can carry our Lord to, more in need. And that mother should be on your calling list for as long as needed.

When our son-in-law died, the time of the funeral was somewhat of a problem to his father. While speaking on the phone with my son, Keith, the father asked, "What would you do?" Keith answered, "Be here." That is my answer to you. There is no other answer.

Please believe my urgency and conviction in this. Trust me and accept this, which I know to be a true, real need. At the moment you notice my absence, I am in great need of this healing sacrament. I may be walking around like I'm under control and even tell you over and over that I am doing OK. Don't believe me. When I'm not there, call my home to see if I would like to have you bring communion. Don't listen to me if I tell you I don't want to put you to the bother. Ask me if you could just stop by sometime today, if it's convenient. Be very, very pushy. Storm my reluctance. If ever there were a time to overstep your boundaries, this is it. If I could, I would send an urgent memo with this message to all priests and clergy in the world. I can't, so I'll just pray for your acceptance of what I've written.

I've been in this horrible situation two years and I'm now able to go to Mass in control of my emotions. Still, it often takes a great deal of effort to maintain my outward composure, but I do. I am back to the soul sustaining gifts of the sacraments. I missed them greatly when I couldn't have access to them. I believe that the absence of their power left ugly scars on my soul. The scars will heal, but you can prevent these wounds from forming. Be a Good Shepherd and watch for the lamb that has wandered away. You might just save its life and return it to its rightful home.

Do I need, at this time, to listen to long, well meaning but non-comforting prayer? No, I need to hear that you will assault heaven with your prayers on behalf of my dead child, the one I love so much.

Do we need to hear that if only our children had quit smoking, or given up that dangerous life-style, they might have lived? No, we've forgotten most, if not all, their faults the moment they died.

We would like to hear about a favorite time you were in their presence or, if you didn't know them, that you've heard what a good person he or she was. Let us tell you how much we loved them.

Should you tell us that God's will is a mystery? Maybe. More than likely, our hearts will harden at this suggestion. More appropriately, you might say that, even for you, this act is so hard to understand. Maybe later we'll accept this as a mystery, but that is far down the road.

Can you make us understand that we need to accept this crushing death? No. Acceptance is far, far in the future. What might help is to know that God's shoulders are very, very strong and can hold our anger without malice toward us.

We might accept your telling us that our wrath is expected in heaven. Were this snatching of our child's life due to a kidnapper here on earth, our outrage would be considered normal and God would be amazed if we weren't angry. Later, say six months later, if our anger is still acute it might need to be examined.

Don't ever try to tell us you understand and feel our pain; there is not a chance we will buy that idea. Tell us that, from what you've learned from others, this pain is beyond imagination, and you will continue to pray for our healing.

Don't tell us we have to turn to God and accept his comfort. We are probably already sitting on His lap. Instead, tell us that you know the coming weeks, months, and even years will be the toughest we'll ever go through. Tell us you are available to us anytime - and I do mean anytime.

Let us know that you understand we may not have enough control over our emotions in the coming time to attend Mass, and that coming to Mass may not be something we can do very soon.

Offer that, in mercy, our church has allowed for our inability to be among large crowds of people. Tell us that attending daily Mass, if we're able, might serve to fulfill our obligation for now.

Don't say, " I know you can't talk right now, but . . ." Ask us to tell you what happened. We need to repeat this over and over until we believe it.

Don't expect to comfort us much, but instead show us your pain and let us comfort you. That awful composure you hide behind offends our ability to take your help.

Tell us you are frightened that what you say or don't say might do harm. Your inadequacy won't harm us, and your truthfulness might help.

We already know that others will probably say some really stupid things (and probably already have), but give us credit for knowing they meant no harm. We'll even give you a break.

Tell us we are doing OK and assure us that whatever we are thinking is probably normal. We really need to hear that we won't cause any further pain for others with our grief. This may seem like a strange thing to say, but say it anyway.

Don't tell us it wasn't our fault. Guilt already has started its work on us. We will eventually sort out if there really was any true guilt, but this, too, needs time.

In the case of suicide, as with my son, guilt is magnified beyond whatever you could imagine. When I express guilt, don't tell me that you're sure I did all I could. Of course I didn't. We never do all we could do. I will sort this out also, but denying my guilt - real or imagined - has no bearing on its existence. It is real, and to deny it invalidates and erases from my mind any credibility you might have with me.

Take heart and know that just your presence will suffice, even if your need should outweigh ours. I've seen priests stand by feeling totally helpless and still be effective. I believe that God gives you all you need in any situation; otherwise why would He have chosen you to be a priest?

I've addressed this issue to priests but know it would apply to any clergy. Also "the experts" that wrote the book may have never been where I have been. If I need to know about something I'm unsure of, I find the best source to ask. Some things I've written will not apply to all parents. Please notice that this is the first time I've included both parents. I purposely wrote this directed from my point of view because I am unable to address the needs of my husband, Bill. I know they were different from mine. But I felt comfortable using "we" to include other mothers. I've talked with enough of them to accept that our needs may be universal.

One of the first things you could do is call a mother, in the parish, who has lost a child. Why not ask who in the parish would be willing to accept this as a ministry? You'll be surprised at our willingness to put ourselves at your service. I would not have bothered to write this if I didn't feel that a ministry for grief is so badly needed.

I take full responsibility for my grief, and am not saying that clergy or laity will have an impact on our self healing.

What you can do, as Christ's ambassador, is let us know you represent Him and, as He would do, you care.

Thank-you for listening...

Sylvia Hess

June 6, 1995

4:30 am About a month ago I went to California to visit our oldest son, Glenn. He lives in Palo Alto, just south of San Francisco. Our travel plans included leaving his home and going up through the wine country and staying in a bed-and-breakfast for two nights, then returning down the coast to home. The kids had pitched in and paid for my two-night stay and this was to be the first B&B for me. It was run by two wonderful people who made us feel like we were their only and top priority, such wonderful hosts. The inn had a gazebo perched at the edge of a cliff that looked out over the ocean; it was like having a box seat at the very best theater. The power and grace of the ocean consumed my total attention over and over during our stay and, as often as I could be in that box seat, I was.

When we went down the path to the shore, I was even more taken by the ocean's strength. As I sat there on a piece of driftwood, I couldn't help but compare this force to the grief process. Had I stood even 10 feet offshore, I would have been knocked down and had to struggle each time to stand again, over and over. Also I would have been cold and fearful, standing there between waves, waiting for the next assault. Grief is much like this.

I thought about how the past two years have been a gradual walk up the beach, pausing to look back, but well aware that I was going away from the terrible power and pain of grieving. Each short space I have trudged through the sand brought its own pain to these aggravated legs, but each pause renewed my resolve to go on. Before I climbed the steps up to the cliff, I needed a longer rest and a more determined effort to make that final ascent.

I may not be quite at the gazebo yet, and maybe I never will be, but it is in my sight and it looks like a nice place to stop and have a pleasurable rest.

Neither you nor I know what is in store for us in our ongoing and constantly changing lives. Maybe, probably, I will again have to face the beast called grief, but next time I'll know its nickname and be well aware of its various habits. It hates for you to try to hurry past it and trying to ignore it is fruitless. It will only come back again and again to show its dominion over your soul. There seems to be an end to its strength and hold on us though, and it does wear out eventually. It is a healer in its own way and, like bitter medicine, will ultimately do its job.

Yesterday I read back over those early weeks and months and will admit it was a very difficult thing to do. Pain and sorrow once again consumed me, but within a short time I was back to being a fairly normal person again. The times of pain are much less frequent and they don't stay long when they come. Their visits are not met with fear and dread as they once were. I have to compare this to an illness that takes a long, long time to mend.

I had the perfect physician to aid me. His fee was submission and following His direction was His only prescription. With patience without measure He guided me through this long, and for some even, fatal disease called grief. I was not without support and attentive care throughout this long time. I've never seen a doctor knock on anyone's door and say: "May I please come in and heal you?" As with most physicians, you must yourself knock on the door. It opens instantly and wide, but the healing will take time.

Your loss may not be as severe as mine; maybe it's as small as a hurting word from someone you love. All you may need is a kind hand. No problem seems too small to Him and He will give answer to your pain. Office hours are great: 24 hours a day. You can't beat that. Sick people are not always in the best of moods, often cranky and full of self-pity. But God always comes through, if we only ask for care.

I expect to be pleading for answers for the rest of my life, but after each query I know an answer will follow. Certainly more often than not I am amazed at how simple the true answer is. We are given this life to enjoy to its fullest measure, but often times we take on too many of its burdens and fall under the weight. We need to lighten up, send our burden to the healer or, at the very least, ask for guidance as to how to carry our crosses.

~ ~ ~

To some this may come as a welcome request, some will brush it off, some will take it to their hearts, but I truly request your prayers on behalf of my family. I pray for yours, please pray for mine.

Walking Naked

ACKNOWLEDGMENTS

Thank you to all for the prayers and kindnesses that made, and still make, a cushion under my heart. I know that God looks with favor on your efforts.

To Bill, who endured, endured and endured. I didn't always like what he said, but there is no telling what might have happened had he not always been there to say it. His "We have to go on" ran fury through me but, without it, I don't know if I would have.

Thank you to my brother, Duane, who called so very often. Many times, those calls were what got me through the day.

Thank you to Connie, who when I hit her office, always took time to take me upstairs to the break room to tell me I was "really doing well," when we both knew I wasn't.

For Jack and Phyllis I wish I could invent new words that express gratitude. They were here in record time, never left our sides, and were as solid as two rocks. No slip ups, didn't miss a beat and covered everything down to the most seemingly insignificant detail. This is a thank you without end.

Thank you to RoseAnn, who, through those longest of winter months, held my hand, let me ramble on and never told me what I ought to do.

Thank you to people like Dick and Nadine and Jim and Donna who came without words to help us keep our dignity intact.

And I thank my women friends, whom I remember being like shadows, in and out of the house, providing food and support. I can't remember if I said, "Thank you."

Thank you to Lois who said to me, "I know you won't believe this, but someday you'll even be able to be happy again." I accepted that comment like a 15-year-old accepts "Someday you'll realize this is best for you" from a parent. She was dead-center right. Her survival has given me permission and also the courage to survive. We will never be "OK," but we will (as much as I hate these words) "go on."

To Our Children

I've saved my first and foremost thank you till last. This one comes from both of us to our children and, as I start this, I know it's not going to be a walk in the park. This I know need not be written and probably I attempted some type of thank you somewhere back in those early writings, but this one is for me.

More than anything else I want you to know that I value your every breath. For each time you take air in and out of your bodies, I offer a prayer of gratitude. This has nothing to do with life and its rising and falling around us, the raging floods that have gone under some of our bridges or the gentle moving of water that goes on its easy way past the good days. It does have to do with who each of you are.

During the early days when I couldn't do what needed to be done, you were like courageous soldiers who did it for me. Your determined strength was, for Dad and me, the only comfort we were able to rest on. That you have gone through this time without allowing your grief to cause any more pain to us is our finest treasure. Later each of you gave Dad and me everything we needed. You gauged your phone calls with great precision, and each one came at exactly the moment it was needed. You were always here at the right time but gave us each the freedom to learn how to stand on our own two feet again.

Our daughter-in-law deserves more credit than I can express. At no time has she indicated that her place in this family should be altered. She has not missed a family dinner or other event. She is one of "the girls" and I will be ever grateful for her loyal heart. Blood does not a daughter make.

To our trouper sons-in-law we are extremely grateful. Two of you married into this family when things could not have been worse. Over and over again we've been grateful for your rock-hard good characters. Each of you has filled a vast area with your generous heart.

To my grandchildren I want to say a special thank-you for each time you made the choice to make life easy on both yourselves and the rest of us. I know that it's been very hard for each of you and often the pain crept out of you in ways you couldn't understand, but this grandma counts you as the best grandkids ever.

You've all raised being family to new heights. You are each one of the finest caliber and give us pride that can't be measured. (But now, in my usual form, I will add that we are also delighted that you each pay your own rent.)

About The Author

Sylvia Hess is a full-time wife, now living in Arkansas City, KS. She recently experienced the joy of welcoming a new grand-daughter, Addison Jane, to her family. She continues to write everyday.

Walking Naked

Please send _____ copy(s) of
"Walking Naked"
at $11.00 each. My check or money order
for $_____ is enclosed.
(Please add $1.50 per book for postage and handling.)
NO CASH OR CODS PLEASE
Allow 2-4 weeks for delivery.

PLEASE ADDRESS BOOK(S) TO:

Name: _____

Address: _____

Address: _____

City, State, Zip: _____

Address orders and inquiries to:

Syl Say's
P.O. Box 1233
Arkansas City, Kansas 67005

Attention: Kim Beckelhimer or
Sylvia F. Hess

316-442-4185 Voice
316-442-3065 Fax
email: kimb@hit.net

Walking Naked